BASIC
SAILING

☆ BASIC SAILING ☆

By M. B. GEORGE

A COMPREHENSIVE illustrated guide for those who plan to sail or who are now sailing. Presented for quick and easy understanding of the factors that concern the seamanlike handling of small sailing craft.

This book serves as a basis or reference for the amateur, the instructor, experienced yachtsman or writer of articles on the sport of sailing. Care—thought—time—experience—have gone into making it unique, accurate and outstanding. Here, the fundamentals, the necessary basic know-how needed to sail a boat in a proper and seamanlike manner are presented by a modern direct approach through the use of illustrations, diagrams, photographs, and easily read text. The thoughts expressed here are not one man's opinion but a factual expression of just what sailing is and how it is practiced. It is not an attempt to ponder over or wander into the theories and practice of racing and its analogous skills, sense, luck or misfortunes.

MOTOR BOATING & SAILING BOOKS
NEW YORK 1971

☆ B A S I C S A I L I N G ☆

REVISED EDITION

C O N T E N T S

How to recognize the different TYPES of SAILING CRAFT

CHAPTER 1

Sailing craft are classified by the position of their mast or masts, the height of the mast, plus the type of sails (known as the sail plan) they carry. The combination of mast and sails is referred to as a rig.

There are two general types of craft:

      1. single-masted and 2. double-masted

There also are two general sail plans:

      1. jib-headed and 2. gaff-headed

A jib-headed rig is one that has a triangular mainsail, the gaff-headed rig is one with a quadrilateral sail. Exceptions, of course, exist to the above classifications but these exceptions (as of today) are modern variations of sailing work boats of the old days or foreign craft.

Most of the small sailboats of today are single-masted vessels. Most of them are called sloops. Modifications of this sloop rig can be found in sailboards, cutters, sailing dinghies, sailing scows and catamarans. The original term for single-masted small sport sailing craft, without a bowsprit (where all sails and rigging are inboard) is *knockabout*. The term occasionally is heard in reference to some present day sailboats, but is not in general use.

Two-masted vessels are called yawls, ketches, or schooners. Each type is distinguished and readily recognized by two factors (1) the height of the masts and (2) the position of the masts in relation to the extreme after end of the waterline, rudder post, or in some cases the helm, which on all three types is in the same fixed relative position. There is always one tall mast, called the mainmast, and one shorter mast.

On the yawl, sketch B, the shorter mast, called the mizzenmast or sometimes the jigger, is aft of the tiller. It is generally quite short in height as compared to the mainmast.

The ketch, sketch C, differs from a yawl in that the shorter mast, called the mizzenmast, is placed just forward of the helm. It is of greater height than a yawl mizzenmast but always shorter than the mainmast, which generally is located in the same relative position as the mainmast on a yawl.

The schooner, sketch D, differs from the other two types. The shorter mast, called the foremast, is forward of the mainmast.

Most two-masted vessels, regardless of type, are generally of larger size and used for cruising. The prime purpose of having two masts is to split the sail plan into small segments so they can be more easily handled and, also, to keep the boat in sailing balance. Since these craft often venture far from their own snug harbors, the meet all conditions of sea and wind. With light winds and moderate sea, extra sails can be set to keep the craft mov-

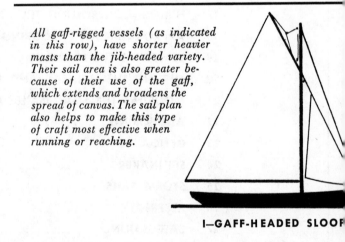

The placement of the mast or masts and their respective, comparative heights are fundamental factors in determining types of vessels. This top row illustrates the mast arrangements of the four most popular types of American sailing craft.

A—SLOOP

Jib-headed craft are the most popular type today because they generally can point higher into the eye of the wind than a gaff rig. The rig is taller and therefore can pick up breezes that are high off the water; besides, there is more driving area in the luff of each sail.

E—JIB-HEADED SLOOP

All gaff-rigged vessels (as indicated in this row), have shorter heavier masts than the jib-headed variety. Their sail area is also greater because of their use of the gaff, which extends and broadens the spread of canvas. The sail plan also helps to make this type of craft most effective when running or reaching.

I—GAFF-HEADED SLOOP

ing. With strong winds and a rough sea the sail area can be easily reduced for safe sailing. The large mainsail can be tightly furled and the boat sailed with only the jib and jigger, as on a yawl, the jib and mizzen as on a ketch, and jib and foresail as on a schooner. A sloop would have to tie in a double reef and perhaps set a storm jib under similar conditions.

Today the yawl is the most popular of the two-masted types though the others have staunch advocates.

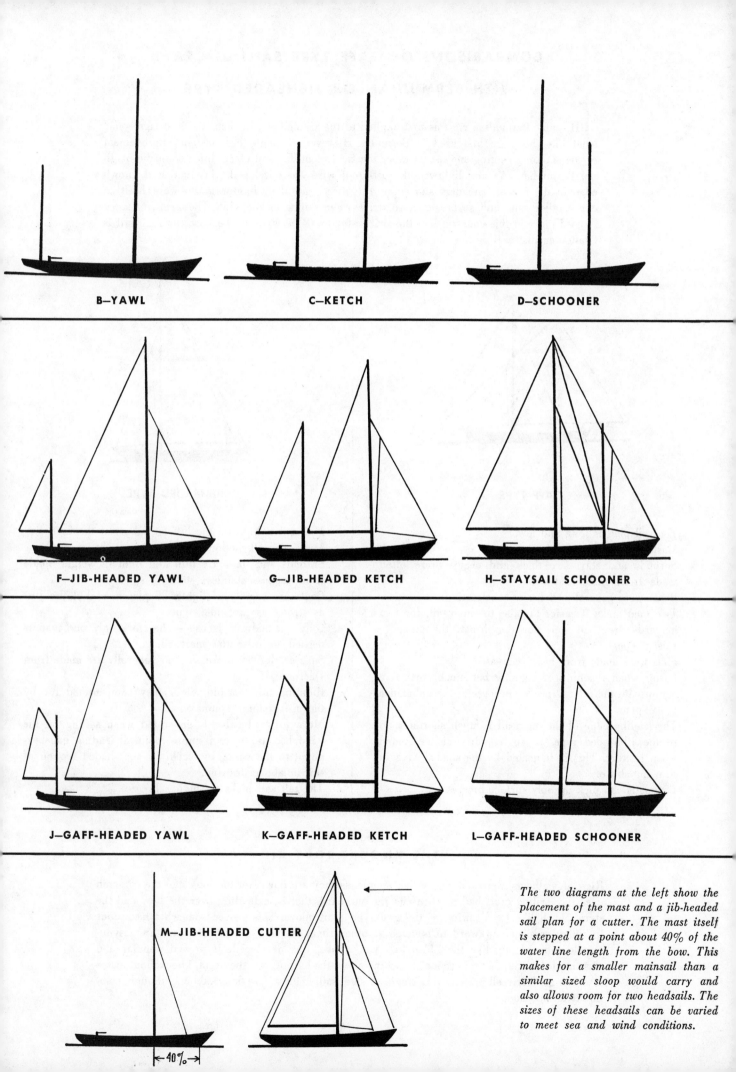

B—YAWL

C—KETCH

D—SCHOONER

F—JIB-HEADED YAWL

G—JIB-HEADED KETCH

H—STAYSAIL SCHOONER

J—GAFF-HEADED YAWL

K—GAFF-HEADED KETCH

L—GAFF-HEADED SCHOONER

M—JIB-HEADED CUTTER

←40%→

The two diagrams at the left show the placement of the mast and a jib-headed sail plan for a cutter. The mast itself is stepped at a point about 40% of the water line length from the bow. This makes for a smaller mainsail than a similar sized sloop would carry and also allows room for two headsails. The sizes of these headsails can be varied to meet sea and wind conditions.

COMPARISONS OF GAFF TYPE SAILING CRAFT

WITH BERMUDIAN OR JIBHEADED TYPE

THE name Bermudian rig was first applied to the triangular sail plans because rigs somewhat like this were first used in Bermuda. However, through the constant improvement of the standing rigging and use of taller masts, present day sail plans differ from the original Bermudian. As new lightweight, rust-proof wire was developed, plus increased knowledge in the use of spreaders and supporting bracing, taller, lighter masts were built to carry taller sails and so create more drive when sailing on the wind. The term *jibheaded* is used more in this country than the British-favored "Bermudian" because the mainsail is triangular like a jib.

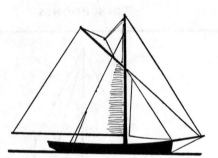

GAFF TYPE

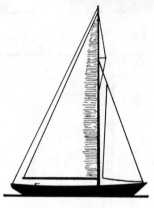

JIBHEADED TYPE

The sail plan is long and low.
Masts are short and heavy.
Shrouds and stays are thick and heavy—were often made from galvanized wire.
Boats were generally of heavy construction.
Two men make it easier to raise the mainsail, for two halyards are used—one for the throat, the other to raise the peak.
Sails were made from heavy canvas.
Faster when reaching or running but much corrective action with the tiller is needed because of the imbalance of sail plan.
The leading edge of the mainsail is much shorter than in the jibheaded type, hence less drive is generated when beating. This is indicated by the shaded area in drawing above.
Low sails can pick up only surface breezes.

Mainsail is high on the luff and short at the foot.
Masts are tall, hollow and light in weight.
Shrouds and stays are thin and light in weight, made from rustless stainless steel.
Boats are usually of lighter displacement but are just as strong as the older type.
Only one halyard is used—therefore only one man is needed to raise the mainsail.
Sails are lighter in weight and generally are made from Dacron.
Running and reaching deficiency compensated for by the use of large spinnakers.
More forward drive is generated when sailing on the wind because there is more mainsail leading edge exposed to the wind. Indicated by the shaded section of sail in above drawing.
The tall sail picks up higher breezes.

THE KNOCKABOUT RIG

Rigs of sailboats were not always as simple as they are now. Not too long ago the common everyday sailing craft had much of its rig outboard, that is, extending over the bow and the stern, much like the drawing of the gaff type craft above. This proved somewhat hazardous in rough seas and awkward to manage at other times. Over a period of years an easy-to-handle inboard rig, like the jibheaded type, above, was developed. It proved popular and was used for Sunday afternoon knocking-about-the-harbor, so the term knockabout came into being. Nearly all present day, single masted sailing craft are knockabouts, though commonly termed sloops.

THE EXTENDED SAIL PLAN

To accommodate an extended sail plan, some craft have a projection extending from the bow called a bowsprit, and at the stern a projection called a boomkin. The bowsprit holds the headstay and/or jibstay and the boomkin holds the backstay on some sloops. On yawls it holds blocks through which the mizzensheet is led.

To keep the bowsprit from breaking when an excessive strain is put on it, a wire or chain is led from the tip of the bowsprit to the stem just above the water line. This chain is called a bobstay.

Should the bowsprit be long, a fixed spar is often used that comes down from the point of the bow to the bobstay. This spar or *spreader* is called a dolphin striker. It probably got its name during the old sailing ship days when dolphins would swim around the bow of a vessel. This projection, when the ship plunged up and down, seemed to strike at the dolphins.

The boomkin is usually a thick oak plank, though sometimes two planks are used extending to form a V. To keep this boomkin from breaking or bending upward, a wire is led downward from its outer end to a point just above the waterline. This wire is called a bob stay.

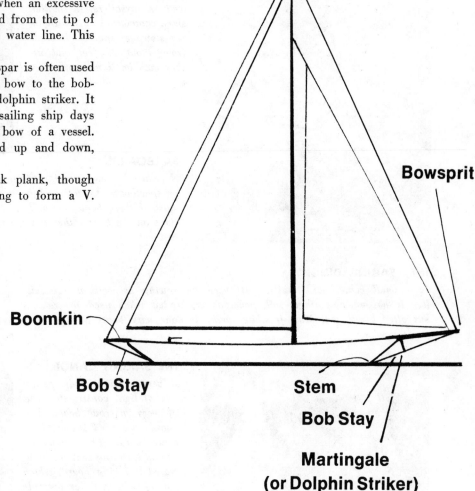

Bowsprit

Boomkin

Bob Stay

Stem

Bob Stay

**Martingale
(or Dolphin Striker)**

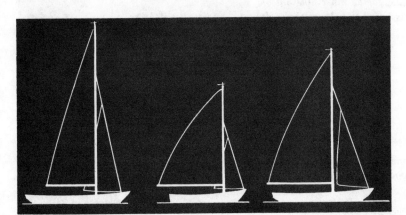

HIGH ASPECT RATIO   LOW ASPECT RATIO   MODERATE ASPECT RATIO

ASPECT RATIO

Aspect ratio *is a term used to describe the relationship of the lengths of luff and foot. A sail with a high luff and short foot is said to have a high aspect ratio; one with a short luff and long foot has a low aspect ratio. A sail not high at the luff and not too short at the foot has a moderate aspect ratio.*

OTHER COMMON TYPES OF SAILBOATS

THE CATAMARAN

Although catamarans may take any type of rig, most of them appear either in sloop or cat rig. These lightweight, high-performance boats are especially popular for racing, though many catamarans serve well as daysailers. In smaller sizes, catamarans have little or no stowage space, although from about 25 feet and up they may be rigged for cruising.

SAILBOARDS

A relatively new—and increasingly popular—type of sailboat is the sailboard or sportboat, characterized by a single lateen-style sail and a low hull. On most of these boats, a small foot well comprises the only cockpit—the crew rides on the boat rather than in it. Sailboards are fast, exciting, demanding, and wet.

THE SAILING DINGHY

Is a small centerboard utility craft used for rowing as well as for sailing. It has a small single sail, generally jib-headed when used for racing, but often lug-rigged. Most frostbite racing is done with boats of this type.

THE SAILING CANOE

A very sensitive craft generally of light construction and of very narrow beam. Lee boards are used instead of a centerboard. The helmsman sits on a sliding seat or board, called a hiking board, which can be extended far overside when necessary to keep the craft upright in strong winds. The helmsman must be quite agile, for he must hike out on this board to balance the craft.

THE CATBOAT

Has the mast forward close to the bow. There is one huge mainsail, generally gaff-headed. It does not carry a jib. The name originally referred to a type of beamy centerboard craft distinctive in hull and rig.

COMET

Overall length .....16' 0"
Waterline (approx.) 14' 3"
Beam .... 5' 0"
Sail area ......136 sq. ft.

THISTLE

Overall length ......17' 0"
Waterline (approx.) 17' 0"
Beam .... 6' 0"
Sail area .....175 sq. ft.

FEW OF THE SAILING CLASSES

SUNFISH

Overall length .....13' 10"
Beam ....4' ½"
Sail area ....75 sq. ft.
Weight ....139 lbs.

SNIPE

Overall length 15' 6"
Waterline ....13' 0"
Beam .... 5' 0"
Sail area ..103 sq. ft.

BLUE JAY

Overall length .....13' 6"
Waterline ....11' 5"
Beam .... 5' 2"
Sail area ....90 sq. ft.

LIGHTNING

Overall length .....19' 0"
Waterline (approx.) 15' 3"
Beam ....6' 6¼"
Sail area ......177 sq. ft.

Small Boat MAINSAILS

CHAPTER 2

No SINGLE item contributes as much to the speed and movement of a boat as do the sails. Therefore, knowledge of their parts, how and what they are made of, and their use is of basic importance.

The object of this chapter is to acquaint you with these factors.

A sail is composed of many widths of material neatly sewn together to a prescribed size and shape. This shape is reinforced at the edges by an extra thin strip of material called a tabling, and at the corners by pieces called reinforcing patches. Roping on one, two, or three edges, depending on the type of sail, is then sewn to the edge of the sail. This sewing of the rope to the sail is of most importance for it controls to quite a degree the set of the sail. The sailmaker, according to his own formula, takes a set number of stiches per foot of canvas to bind the fabric to the rope and while so doing takes in extra material. This is necessary to counteract the excessive stretch of rope as compared to cloth. It also serves to create the curve or shape the sail will take when hoisted. The relationships between stitches of canvas to foot of rope are sailmakers' secrets.

Countless experiments and experiences, over many, many years, in cutting and breaking in new canvas (cotton) sails brought them to a wonderful degree of efficiency. Canvas sails are slowly, gently, carefully broken in so that they will be wrinkle-free, enabling the wind to flow without interruption over their surfaces.

Until a few years ago most sails were made from special grades of finely woven Egyptian cotton. Now a synthetic material, Dacron, has come to the fore and has proved most effective. Nylon has also been tried, with success where a certain amount of stretch is acceptable.

The principal sails on a small single-masted boat are the mainsail, the jib and the spinnaker.

MAINSAILS

There are three types of mainsails: the jib-headed (also called the Marconi and Bermudian), the gaff-headed, and

---

COMPARISON OF CANVAS AND DACRON SAILS

CANVAS
—must be carefully and slowly broken in (not pulled out of shape) so that their contours will be free from wrinkles
—shrink in wet or damp weather
—are cut smaller when first made, to allow for stretch and breaking in to required dimension
—manila rope is used to reinforce the luff and foot of these except for headsails (on big boats) where wire is used
—proved through many, many years of use
—may rot if stowed when wet

DACRON
—can be used immediately, no breaking in period required
—practically unaffected by dampness
—often are full of wrinkles yet these wrinkles do not seem to impair the sails effectiveness
—light and very strong
—cloth, rope and stitching thread are all made from one material (Dacron) thereby eliminating any difference in stretch or shrinkage
—have a hard, shiny finish
—are slightly more expensive than canvas

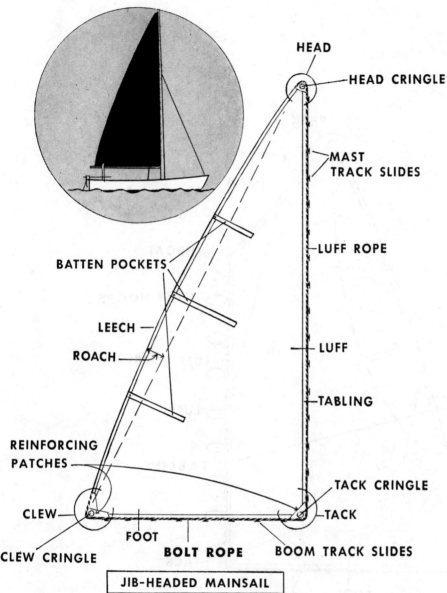

HEAD

HEAD CRINGLE

MAST TRACK SLIDES

LUFF ROPE

BATTEN POCKETS

LUFF

LEECH

ROACH

TABLING

REINFORCING PATCHES

TACK CRINGLE

CLEW

TACK

FOOT

CLEW CRINGLE

BOLT ROPE

BOOM TRACK SLIDES

JIB-HEADED MAINSAIL

As readily seen in this drawing, the jib-headed mainsail is long, narrow, and triangular in shape. Its popularity is due to the ease of handling (only one halyard needed to raise it) and its wonderful "on the wind" ability. The majority of small boats use this type of sail for their main driving sail. Another characteristic is that the trailing edge (called the leech), is the only side of the sail that does not have a reinforcing rope sewn to it. The leech is also cut in a long curve, from head to clew, that allows for a certain fullness. This extra material as indicated between the dotted straight line and the leech itself, gives extra drive to the sail when reaching or running. It is called the roach. Because the roach is apt to sag or flap in the wind it is held straight and stiff by thin, narrow, smoothly finished slats made from flexible hard wood, or plastic, called battens. Battens are tied tight in the batten pockets otherwise they would fly out and away when pressure of the wind is exerted on them.

All relative parts of all sails are similarly named, whether the sail is a mainsail, a jib or a spinnaker (with slight exceptions on the gaff mainsail and the spinnaker).

The leading edge is the luff.
The trailing edge is the leech.
The lower edge is the foot.
The top corner is the head.
The lower leading corner is the tack.
The trailing after corner is the clew.

the loose-footed. The jib-headed mainsail is by far the most commonly used in the U.S.A. It is shaped like a long right angle triangle.

The gaff-head mainsail is a four-sided (quadrilateral-shaped) sail on which the upper edge is fastened to a spar called a gaff, hence its name.

The third type of mainsail is called loose-footed. Its general shape is similar to the other mains, but its foot

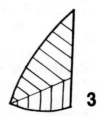

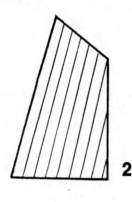

Common cuts for three types of mainsails:
1. diagonal, or "cross-cut," 2. vertical,
3. mitre-cut.

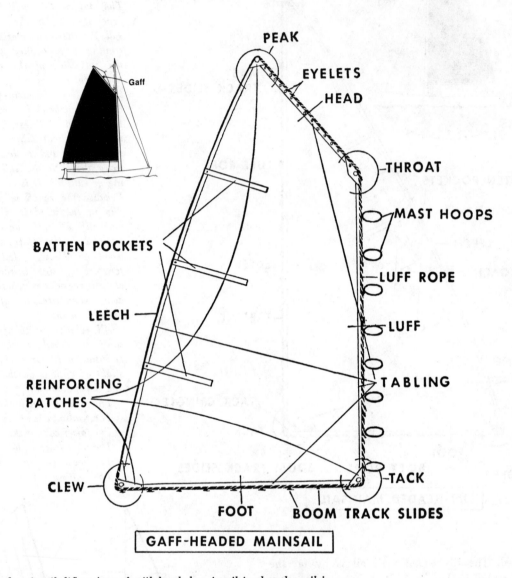

PEAK

EYELETS

HEAD

THROAT

MAST HOOPS

LUFF ROPE

LUFF

TABLING

Gaff

BATTEN POCKETS

LEECH

REINFORCING PATCHES

CLEW

TACK

FOOT

BOOM TRACK SLIDES

GAFF-HEADED MAINSAIL

The gaff-headed mainsail differs from the jib-headed mainsail in that the sail is quadrilateral. It also is longer on the foot and much shorter along the luff, and its sail area generally is much greater. The fourth or high side of this sail is called the head and it is fastened by lashings to a spar called a gaff, from which the sail gets its name. The highest outside corner of the sail is called the peak and the top corner of the luff close to the mast is called the throat. The sail is raised by two halyards. One is called a throat halyard (it raises the throat) and the other is called the peak halyard because it controls the set of the peak when the gaff is raised. The parts of this sail are named in the accompanying drawing. The other parts, except for the distinguishing characteristics, mentioned above, are named exactly as on the jib-headed mainsail shown on the previous page.

In this country the gaff-headed mainsail, or variation thereof, came first. It was used on both pleasure craft and the then much more numerous sailing work boats. The gaff-headed main was used until the taller jib-headed mainsail proved itself more efficient and easier to handle. When proper staying was designed for the tall masts necessary for this type of sail, the gaff-headed mainsail rapidly lost favor. However, there are still some small one-design classes and cruising yachts that use this sail.

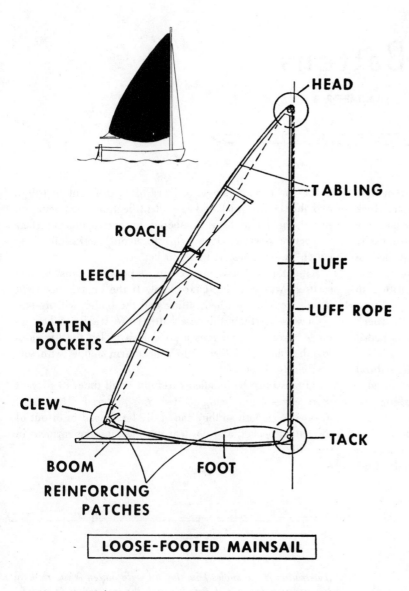

HEAD

TABLING

ROACH

LEECH

LUFF

BATTEN POCKETS

LUFF ROPE

CLEW

TACK

BOOM

FOOT

REINFORCING PATCHES

LOOSE-FOOTED MAINSAIL

The loose footed mainsail is so named because the foot or lower edge of the sail hangs free and is not fastened by lacings or slides to a boom. This lower edge does not have a bolt rope and is finished in a manner similar to a leech. The set or curvature of the sail, whether full or flat, is controlled by a line that is tied to the clew and runs to an outhaul on the boom. Besides the regular batten pockets in the leech, there often is a batten pocket sewn in the foot to keep this lower edge from curling up. This sail is currently used by many of the small dinghy classes.

or lower edge is not fastened; it hangs loose. It is controlled by a single line fastened to the clew and pulled out by a line attached to the end of the boom, or by an outhaul.

JIBS

Originally, the sail that we call a jib was named a stay-sail. Old-timers who still call it by that name are technically correct. Jibs were set from the bowsprit of the old-time sailing vessel. The staysail was inboard and nearest the mast. Today, practically everyone calls the single sail forward of the mast of a small sloop, a jib.

There are several different types of jib: the working jib, the genoa jib, the storm jib, and others. The first two named are of prime importance because they are in constant everyday use.

The working jib, triangular in shape, is the ordinary average-sized sail that fits in the triangle formed by the mast, the foredeck and the jibstay.

The genoa jib is a huge triangular-shaped sail that overlaps the mast.

The storm jib is a small sail in comparison to others, made of very heavy material to withstand storm winds.

THE SPINNAKER

The spinnaker is comparatively the latest and newest development in sails. It replaces the jib when broad reaching or sailing before the wind. It is huge and bulbous-shaped, and made from the lightest of materials so that it can puff or billow out in the lightest of winds. It flies out and up, outside of the headstay. An additional pole is carried (called a spinnaker boom) to hold a lower corner out to catch the wind. The other corner's movements are controlled by a sheet.

Battens

BATTENS are long, thin, narrow slats made from fine-grained oak or ash, plastics or aluminum. They are thick at the outer end and taper to the other. All edges are rounded and smooth so that the batten can be slipped easily in and out of its pocket in the sail. A hole is drilled in the heavier end so that a short line, called a batten tie, can be passed through it. This is to hold the batten in place and keep it from slipping out of its pocket.

The purpose of battens is to keep the leech and the roach even and straight so that the flow of wind is not impeded as it passes over the sail.

They should be flexible enough to yield with the natural curve of the sail. If the batten is too stiff it causes an edge or bend to form in the canvas, thereby disturbing the smooth flow of wind.

Pockets for battens, sewn in the sail, should be at least an inch or two longer and slightly wider than the battens themselves so as to allow the battens to work and adjust to the pressure exerted on them.

Battens for any single sail are often different in length and should, for quick and easy identification when being inserted, be lettered or numbered to correspond to their respective pockets. This helps to avoid confusion as to which batten goes in what pocket.

After the batten is inserted in its pocket it must be tied securely with a tight square knot. If the knot is not tight it will work loose when sailing and the batten will fly out.

Because of their thinness battens are fragile. When removed from the sail it is a good idea to lay the flat sides together and bind them into a neat firm bundle with several elastic bands.

Battens must be handled carefully at all times to prevent their edges from being dented or splintered. They must always be smooth so they can easily be slipped in or out of the batten pocket, and not tear or cause uneven surfaces in the sail.

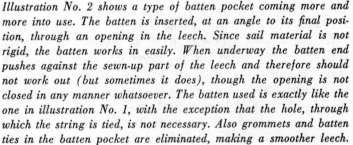

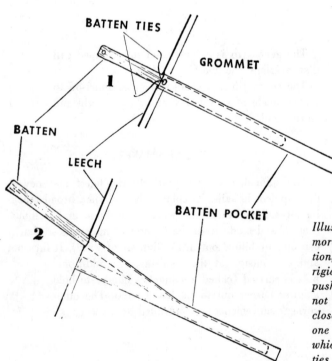

Illustration No. 1 shows how the old-style batten is inserted in its pocket, narrow end fist. When fully inserted it is tied in place by two small pieces of line called batten ties. These pass through the grommets in the sail and the hole in the batten. They are then formed into a square knot. Tying a tight hard knot is most important, for a loose knot will open when wind pressure is exerted on the sail, and a flapping leech will cause the batten to fly out of its pocket.

Illustration No. 2 shows a type of batten pocket coming more and more into use. The batten is inserted, at an angle to its final position, through an opening in the leech. Since sail material is not rigid, the batten works in easily. When underway the batten end pushes against the sewn-up part of the leech and therefore should not work out (but sometimes it does), though the opening is not closed in any manner whatsoever. The batten used is exactly like the one in illustration No. 1, with the exception that the hole, through which the string is tied, is not necessary. Also grommets and batten ties in the batten pocket are eliminated, making a smoother leech.

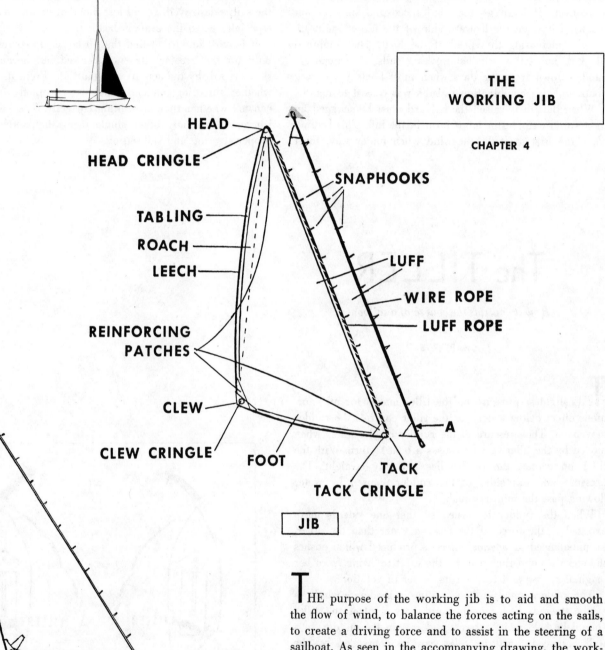

HEAD

HEAD CRINGLE

TABLING

ROACH

LEECH

REINFORCING
PATCHES

CLEW

CLEW CRINGLE

FOOT

SNAPHOOKS

LUFF

WIRE ROPE

LUFF ROPE

A

TACK
TACK CRINGLE

JIB

CLUB

This illustration shows how a club is generally fastened to the foot of a jib. It can also be fastened to the sail by sail slides similar to the slides on a main boom. Some clubs run the entire length of the foot and others are a foot or two shorter. Their purpose is to make a jib self-tacking and controllable by a single sheet.

THE purpose of the working jib is to aid and smooth the flow of wind, to balance the forces acting on the sails, to create a driving force and to assist in the steering of a sailboat. As seen in the accompanying drawing, the working jib is triangular in shape and its parts are named exactly like those of a jib-shaped mainsail. It fits in the area between the mast, jibstay and deck. Its tack is fastened close to the deck at the jibstay to which the snaphooks, or hanks, on the jib luff are attached.

Most jibs are loose-footed and their curvature is controlled by jib sheets and the placement of the jib sheet leads. An exception is found when a short spar called a club is used to keep the foot straight. Some cruising yachts, but few racing classes, use this arrangement.

The leech, more often than not, has battens to keep it straight and prevent the sail from curling. This is very important; if the leech be allowed to curl it will force the wind flowing off the jib to strike the leeward side of the mainsail (called backwinding). This modifies the forces created and defeats one purpose of the jib.

A jib should aid and not destroy the forces creating drive. A jib that sets well always helps the performance of a mainsail. It increases the wind speed and smooths out the wind flow on the leeward side of the larger mainsail, thereby increasing the speed of the boat. The combined jib and mainsail are called working sails, an expression handed down from the days when most boats were work boats and this combination of sails was easiest to handle.

When the jib is raised the halyard must be snugged up tight so no wrinkles or loops form in the luff. This leading edge, the first to strike the wind when under way, must always be kept bar-taut. Sometimes (see A in illustration) a wire is used instead of a luff rope. This aids in keeping the luff straight and also eliminates some of the vertical strain from the canvas. When this arrangement is used loops are spliced in the wire at the head and tack. The tack cringle and head cringle then are not necessary so are left out of the sail plan. Should the luff hang loose, or the forestay to which it is fastened hang slack, the shape of the sail is destroyed. It will lose much of its driving power, especially when the craft is beating.

It is most important that the jib be set up correctly, not only for the greater efficiency derived but because most skippers sail by the actions of a taut luff. From its actions, whether shivering, violently shaking, or quietly full, they can tell whether they are sailing correctly. The luff of the jib more than any other single factor holds the key to proper steering and sail-setting.

The TILLER

How it controls the course of a sailboat

CHAPTER 5

THE slightest pressure on the tiller makes for an enormous effect below water, for the tiller controls the rudder movement. The pressure of the rudder on the water when moved by the tiller is what causes a boat to turn. With the tiller on center, the rudder lies perfectly straight. The pressure on both sides of the rudder, caused by water flowing past the hull, is equal.

When the rudder is turned so that one side is more exposed to the force of the flowing water than the other, an unbalanced or unequal effect is produced which pushes the stern around thus causing the craft to swing from her original course and turn on its center of rotation.

The modern small sailboat, sailing in moderate winds, is easily steered. For sensitive and easy control the tiller should be held at its extreme end, not in the middle. In a well balanced craft the tiller can be controlled by the finger tips when sailing to windward.

When the wind increases and the boat is reaching, a firm grip is necessary.

In steering, the tiller should never be jerked back and forth. Steering movements should be smooth, the less movement the better, for the turned rudder has a retarding effect on the speed of the boat.

The tiller is always moved in a direction opposite to that in which the bow is to move or direction to be steered. If the boat is to go to port, the tiller is moved to starboard; if it is to go to starboard, the tiller is moved to port.

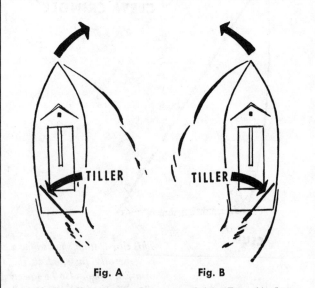

Fig. A   **Fig. B**

If the tiller is moved to port (left) (Fig. A) the bow turns to starboard (right). If the tiller is moved to starboard (right) (Fig. B) the bow turns to port (left). The craft always turns in a direction opposite to that in which the tiller is moved.

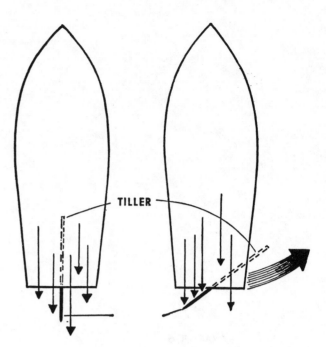

When the tiller and rudder are in line with the keel (amidships) in the left diagram, the water flows evenly and easily by the rudder. When the tiller is moved, causing the rudder to interfere with the even stream of water flowing under the keel, (right diagram), a pressure is created against the side of the rudder. This pressure causes the stern to swing and the craft to turn on its center of rotation. Water flows over the rudder in much the same manner as wind over a sail and with the same resultant effects. There is an angle of rudder giving the greatest turning effect for each particular boat. If turned at a greater angle, the rudder gives more braking action, less turning. If the rudder is positioned at full 90° to the keel, it acts mostly as a brake and does little turning.

THE TILLER EXTENSION

A TILLER extension is a pivoting bar fastened to the end of the tiller to facilitate steering when it becomes necessary for the skipper to be out on the rail in strong winds. It eliminates stretching and reaching to man the tiller.

The bar is fastened to the tiller in a manner that allows it to swivel or turn to either side, forward and aft, a full 360°. When turned aft, it lays snugly on top of the tiller and gives an appearance of being part of the tiller.

The fittings holding the bar must be somewhat tight (not loose) so that any movement of the bar is instantly transmitted to the tiller. The extension itself should reach approximately from the tiller, when it is on center, to the rail. This allows for an easy hold when leaning out over the rail. It should be made of a strong hard wood such as oak, ash or mahogany.

Many skippers work out ingenious ways of fastening the bar to the tiller. In its simplest form this fitting is a screw bolt, a washer and a countersunk nut, with the bolt cut to the combined thickness of both bar and tiller. (See illustration.)

Should the bolt extend beyond the lower edge of the tiller it may snag any loose line. This arrangement may occasionally work loose but it can easily be tightened by a few turns of a screw driver, thereby retaining the stiff swivel action necessary when in use.

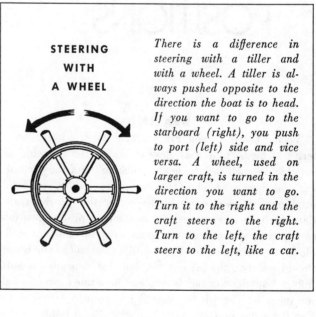

STEERING WITH A WHEEL

There is a difference in steering with a tiller and with a wheel. A tiller is always pushed opposite to the direction the boat is to head. If you want to go to the starboard (right), you push to port (left) side and vice versa. A wheel, used on larger craft, is turned in the direction you want to go. Turn it to the right and the craft steers to the right. Turn to the left, the craft steers to the left, like a car.

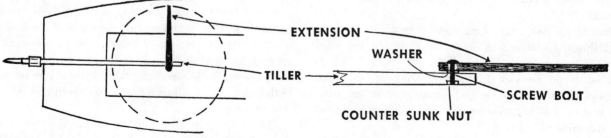

An example of a simple and easily made tiller extension.

CHAPTER 6

The BASIC SAILING POSITIONS

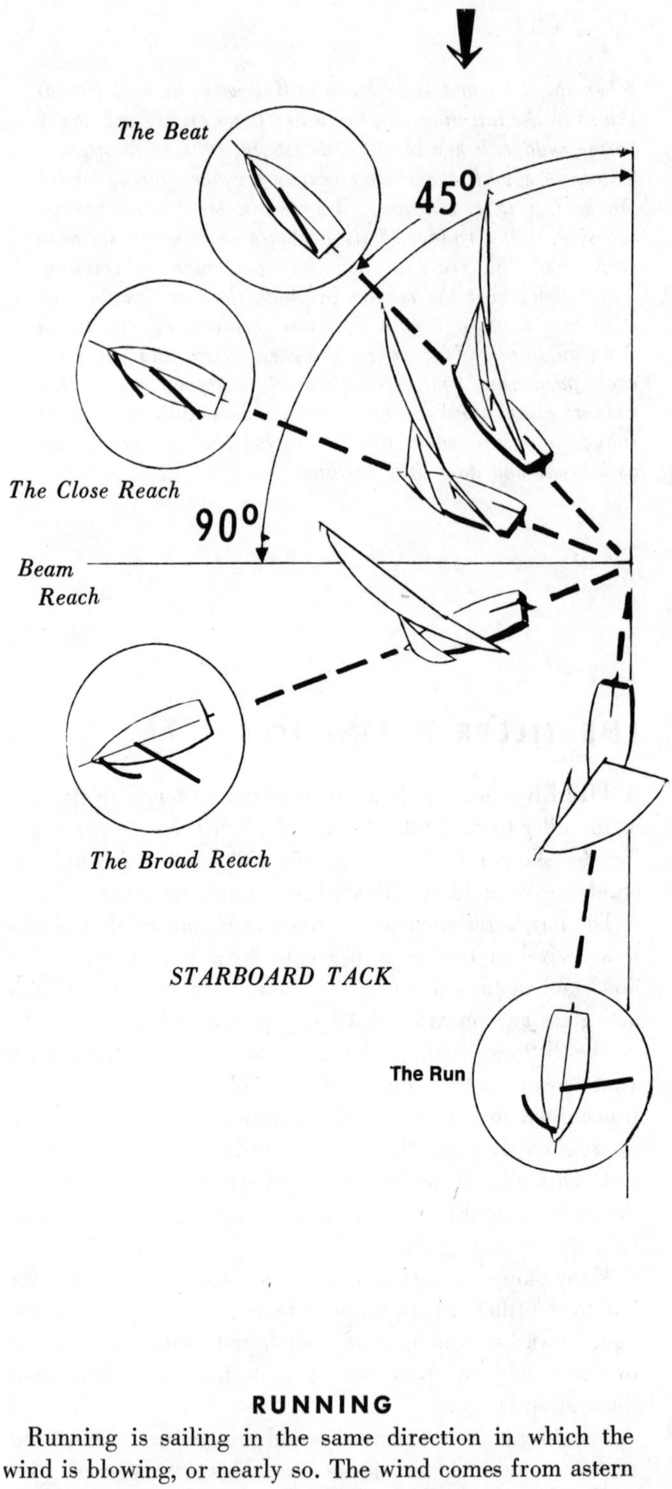

BEATING

When "beating" you are working to windward in a series of tacks, sailing as close to the eye of the wind as possible on each tack without "pinching" and thus retarding the boat's speed. The sheets are hauled in hard bringing the boom close to the center line of the craft. Care must be taken to get the boom in a proper position so the craft will sail at its maximum speed and not stall. More often than not, for better sailing, the end of the boom should point to the lee quarter, but that depends on how full or how flat the sail is cut, and how much breeze and sea there is. The jib too should be carefully trimmed so that it creates maximum draft on the leeward side of the mainsail.

Generally a boat can sail no closer than 45° to the true wind direction. Of course, some sail closer to the wind than 45°, others do not do as well.

Sails should be kept full and drawing at all times. Keeping the proper sailing angle in relation to the wind and course calls for sensitive tiller handling and skillful sail trimming.

When trimmed for beating, a boat is said to be *on the wind* or *close hauled*.

The Beat

45°

The Close Reach

90°

Beam Reach

The Broad Reach

STARBOARD TACK

The Run

RUNNING

Running is sailing in the same direction in which the wind is blowing, or nearly so. The wind comes from astern or slightly on the quarter. It is the slowest point of sailing when the wind is very light.

The mainsail is set by letting out sheet until the boom is nearly at right angles to the center line of the boat. The whole sail then presents a broad front to the wind and most of the driving force is derived from the push of the wind against it. Theoretically the sail should be set at 90° to the wind but actual trim has to take speed and sail shape into account.

The working jib does not set or function too well on this point of sailing since it is blanketed by the mainsail. It slaps or swings back and forth unless held out by a pole.

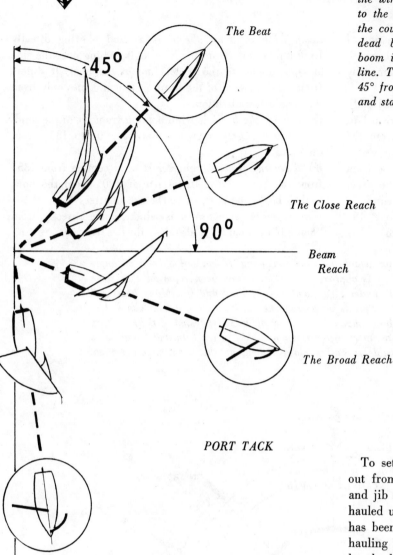

The Beat

45°

The Close Reach

90°

Beam
Reach

The Broad Reach

PORT TACK

The trimming of sail is governed by wind direction and its relation to the course sailed. The closer the craft has to sail to the wind the closer the boom is brought to the center line of the boat. The more the course of the craft approaches a run dead before the wind, the further the boom is eased off away from the center line. The upper portion of the diagram, 45° from the eye of the wind on both port and starboard tack, cannot be sailed.

The spinnaker was invented and perfected for use when running or broad reaching and supplants the inefficient working jib on these points of sailing. It noticeably increases the speed of the boat.

Running is also called "sailing before the wind" and the term "wind aft" relates to this point of sailing.

Close Reach, Beam Reach, and *Broad Reach* are all intermediate points of sailing between that of *on the wind* and *running.*

When wind comes from a point directly abeam the boat is on a *beam reach.*

When wind comes from directions between that of a beam reach and a beat the craft is then *close reaching.*

A boat is said to be sailing a *broad reach* when wind comes from directions between that of a run and a beam reach.

CLOSE REACH

To set sails for a close reach the sheets should be let out from a close-hauled position until both the mainsail and jib start to flutter along the luff. Both sheets are then hauled until the fluttering stops. If the releasing of sheets has been done slowly and carefully only a few inches of hauling is necessary. The craft will move faster and have less heel than when sailing to windward close-hauled.

BEAM REACH

When wind is abeam or close to it a craft is said to be sailing on a "beam reach." The handling of sail is exactly the same as when sailing on a close or a broad reach. When sails are properly set in relation to one another and at the correct angle to the wind it is the fastest point of sailing for some types; schooners like it a bit farther aft.

BROAD REACH

You are *broad reaching* when the wind is coming from slightly abaft the beam to a point on the quarter. Here again, after the craft has been put on course, the sheets are let out until the luffs of the sails start to flutter. The sheets then are hauled in enough to stop the fluttering. Only a few inches of hauling are necessary. Broad reaching is the easiest point of sailing as the craft appears to be more in balance, though care must be exercised in keeping the sails at their full drawing angle to the wind. The boom generally is kept at an approximate angle half way between the center line of the boat and the direction the wind pennant is pointing.

RELATION of WIND to a MOVING BOAT

CHAPTER 7

Wind as we generally know comes from a direction of a point on the compass, and is called North wind, South wind, East wind or West wind. Wind is always named by the direction from which it comes.

However, in relation to a moving boat, wind has additional names. Wind comes from ahead, from forward of the beam, from abeam, from abaft the beam, from the quarter and from astern (wind aft).

A head wind or wind ahead is any wind coming from ahead within 45° on either side of the bow. The exact point from which it comes is called the eye of the wind.

Wind from forward of the beam is any wind between 45° on either side of the bow to almost directly abeam.

Beam wind or wind abeam is a wind blowing directly from a point 90° from the bow. It is coming over the side at right angles to the center line of the boat. It differs from wind forward of the beam in that it comes only from this one exact direction.

Wind abaft the beam is wind coming from aft of the 'midships line, roughly anywhere between 90° to 135° from the bow.

Wind coming from the quarter is wind coming from 135° from the bow to directly astern or 180° from the bow, said to be on the port, or starboard, quarter.

Wind coming from astern is wind coming directly from "behind" the boat. It is also described as *wind aft*.

A boat cannot sail in the direction from which the wind is coming. It can sail only at an angle to it. The closest practical sailing angle is approximately 45°. It has been reported that some boats sail as close to the wind as 33° under ideal conditions of wind and sea. Many boats sail at an angle greater than 45°. The 45° angle is an average figure. How close a boat can sail to the wind depends on a number of factors, among them the set of the sails, design of the hull, trim of the boat, strength of the wind, smoothness of the water and skill of the helmsman. Sailing as close to the eye of the wind as possible is sailing close hauled, on the wind, pointing high.

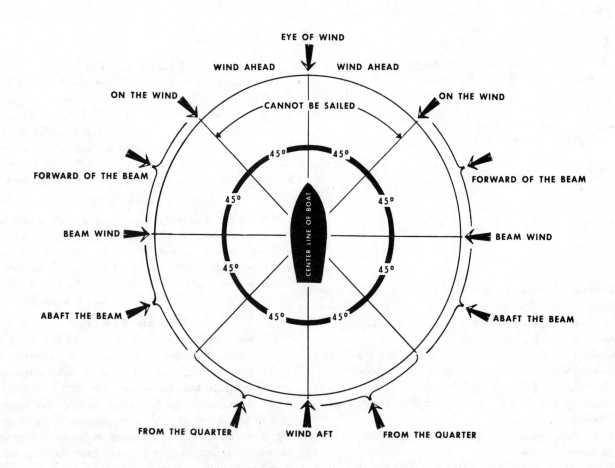

The diagram above illustrates the names of the winds in relation to a moving boat. Notice the sectors are separated every 45° and are similar in proportion to the major divisions on a compass.

VEERING AND BACKING

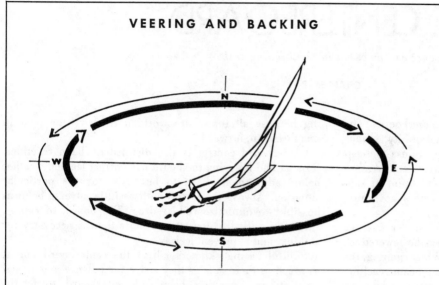

WHEN wind direction changes in relation to the horizon it either VEERS or BACKS. It is said to VEER when it changes or swings to the right or clockwise. It is said to BACK when it swings to the left or counter clockwise. Thus if the wind has been blowing from the North and swings around to the East it is *veering*. If it swings the other way, to the west, it is *backing*.

HAULING AND VEERING

To describe a change in wind direction in relation to the craft itself, the terms HAUL and VEER are used. When the wind changes direction to come from a point more towards the bow the wind is said to HAUL. When it changes direction to come from a point more toward the stern it is said to VEER. As an illustration: You are sailing a predetermined course on a beam reach. The wind suddenly changes and comes from a more forward direction, causing you to haul in sheet. It is then said that the wind has HAULED. If the wind comes from a direction more toward the stern, causing you to let out sheet, it is said that the wind has VEERED.

OFFICIAL DESIGNATIONS OF STRENGTH OF WINDS

STRENGTH of winds are designated in three ways: 1) by Beaufort Scale Number; 2) by National Weather Service designations; and 3) by velocity in miles per hour.

BEAUFORT SCALE	NATIONAL WEATHER SERVICE DESIGNATIONS	VELOCITY IN MILES PER HOUR
0	CALM	0 to 1
1	LIGHT AIR	1 to 3
2	LIGHT BREEZE	4 to 7
3	GENTLE BREEZE	8 to 12
4	MODERATE BREEZE	13 to 18
5	FRESH BREEZE	19 to 24
	Small boat sailors must be careful in handling sails and use of helm.	
6	STRONG BREEZE	25 to 31
	Much too strong for small boats to be sailing. Stay at the mooring.	
7	MODERATE GALE	32 to 38
8	FRESH GALE	39 to 46
9	STRONG GALE	47 to 54
10	WHOLE GALE	55 to 63
	Haul boat out of the water.	
11	STORM	64 to 73
12	HURRICANE	74 and over

WHEN the winds are of greater intensity than a strong breeze, small-boat skippers should check mooring gear to insure the safety of the boat. When warned by the weather bureau of the approach of an extremely strong blow, boats in exposed anchorages should be hauled out, if possible, and protected from damaging winds and waves. Though a craft may have oversized mooring equipment, the surge of the sea can often upset centerboard boats. Also, there is the threat from craft that have broken loose from their moorings; they can drift down, hit your boat and damage it.

BEAUFORT scale numbers were developed during the great old days of sail. It was the first attempt to officially designate the strengths of winds. This scale is referred to on a world-wide basis, and is used largely by cruising skippers.

THE CENTERBOARD

Its use and functions in small sailing craft

CHAPTER 8

THERE are no hard rules for handling centerboards. The functions of a centerboard are to impart stability, reduce leeway and aid in steering. Different skippers use the centerboard in different ways under similar water and weather conditions. Weight and disposition of crew, point of sailing, hull form and helm response are factors governing position of the centerboard.

In general, when beating to windward under average weather conditions, the centerboard should be lowered all the way for maximum lateral resistance. When running, the board is all the way up. For close reaching, beam reaching or broad reaching, the board is raised to positions between these two extremes with more board down when sailing on a close reach than when broader off. These, as has been pointed out, are general rules; variations on the basic theme are many among experienced sailors.

A lowered board aids steering, helps in keeping a craft from rolling in a seaway, reduces angle of heel, makes sailing a straight course off the wind easier, and reduces leeway; but it adversely affects speed through the water under certain conditions.

The board should be down when beating or close reaching, for here the reduction of leeway is of more importance than speed through water. With the centerboard all the way up, a boat may sail faster, but it will lose distance to windward because of leeway (slide slip) when beating or close reaching. On these points of sailing, with the board up, the angle of heel is increased and the craft will often sail an irregular course, thus requiring frequent helm corrections and inducing rudder drag.

The board is kept all the way up when sailing before moderate winds in smooth water. A slight lowering of the board will help steering and reduce weaving or rolling in rough going. Assuming the craft is kept "on its feet," leeway and angle of heel are not factors in this point of sailing because all forces are working to drive the boat in one direction, forward.

Centerboard control is also dictated by helm reactions. Raising and lowering the board can correct lee and weather helm; adjustments have to be made for the particular situation. Always try to sail with as little adverse helm as possible, to minimize rudder drag. The board, of course, should be raised or lowered no more than is necessary for stability and to prevent leeway.

Skillful racing skippers adjust the centerboard almost as much as their sails as they strive for balance among sail position, crew position, helm and centerboard, to get the best performance from the boat.

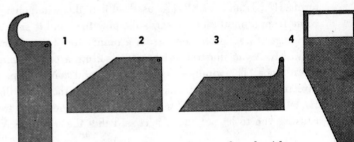

Four common shapes of centerboards (there are many others): 1 is a type generally used on small sailing dinghies and in some one-design classes. The hook at the top is a hand grip, used to lower or raise the board. Friction holds the board in position. 2 and 3 are pivoting types, used on Comet and other one-design class sailboats where up-and-down control is achieved with a pennant and block. 4 is a daggerboard, such as used in the Snipe class. This one is raised and lowered by hand.

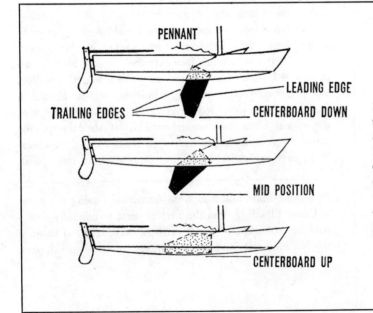

POSITION OF CENTERBOARD

The drawings show the relative positions of a conventional centerboard when the board is lowered all the way, half lowered, and fully raised (board up). The centerboard pennant should be spot-marked by a painted ring or woven colored thread to indicate the amount of board exposed in the water. This can best be done when the craft is out of the water before the sailing season starts.

SHAPE OF LEADING AND TRAILING EDGES OF A CENTERBOARD

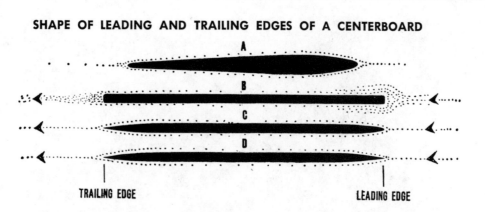

TRAILING EDGE

LEADING EDGE

For best sailing results, centerboards should have carefully shaped edges. Many metal boards come from the foundry with rough, more or less square edges, and are installed that way, despite the fact that it reduces sailing efficiency by building up friction around the plate.

The trailing edge of a centerboard should come to a smoothly tapered knife edge, so that the water flows off with very little disturbance. It should be so sharp that gloves must be worn when handling.

The leading edge must be rounded or sharpened to prevent formation of eddies in that area. Whether it is round or sharp makes little difference in the overall drag, because skin friction along the length of the blade is the controlling factor. To reduce the skin friction, surfaces should be polished smooth. One factor in favor of the more rounded leading edge is that it is not as easily damaged or nicked as a sharp edge.

The drawing above indicates cross sections of typi-cal centerboards. A is a shaped wooden board; B, a metal board with square edges as it comes from the foundry. C and D indicate how B should best be shaped. The dotted lines indicate water flow. Notice the turbulence caused by the blunt ends of B, especially in contrast with the easy flow over C and D. The trailing edge of a streamlined wooden board (A) naturally cannot be worked down as fine as a metal board (if it is to endure). Still, it is a much more efficient board than B. Rounded edges, in themselves, do not make for smooth flow of water if the board is pitted or rough. Centerboards should be smooth, as the bottom of a good hull. Shaped edges, though difficult to maintain because they are easily nicked, and a smooth finish pay off in speed. Some designers of small, very fast planing boats believe that the shape of both wood centerboard and rudder should be the reverse of that of A above, contending that a sharp leading edge is more efficient than the oval.

Much has been done to advance the technique of centerboard handling by skippers of swift planing craft. The International 14-foot dinghy here is sailing at maximum speed as she planes on a broad reach. The faster a craft sails, the less centerboard is needed until the point is reached where the craft sails itself, almost without tiller control. The possibility of capsize then grows.

For maximum control over the boat, essential when rounding racing marks, coming about, jibing, or responding to a luff, the centerboard should be all the way down. With the board in this position, the craft turns sharply on its center of rotation and has a much greater degree of stability than if the board were only part way down.

Changing course with the board up, or only slightly down, permits the boat to slip sideways. A slow, wide turn is the result and the skipper may wonder why his craft does not respond to the helm. In very strong winds he would be in real difficulty and may not be able to turn.

Before making a turn in the course, the centerboard should be lowered on approaching the mark and not adjusted until the craft has settled down on its new course with crew in proper position and all sails trimmed.

TURNING MARK

The solid line in the diagram indicates the course of a boat around a turning mark with the centerboard down. The dotted line indicates how a craft slips off to leeward when the board is up. When racing, another boat sailing properly can nip between the sliding craft and the buoy, thereby gaining a position and the weather berth. In non-competitive sailing, a slide to leeward could put the boat down on another, or onto an obstruction.

HELPFUL HINT:

If a centerboard which ordinarily works easily becomes stuck and cannot be raised or lowered, try sailing off the wind, or rocking the boat while hauling on the centerboard pennant. Strong side pressure on the board when beating or reaching may make the board unresponsive. Sailing downwind releases the pressure while rocking moves the pressure from one side to the other.

Should an object be caught between the board and the trunk, it may be freed by raising the pennant slowly and releasing it quickly several times in succession. If this does not work, get rid of the obstruction; a wire with a hook on one end can be used for probing.

A centerboard is often jerked up sharply and violently so that the fine formed edges bang against the inside top of the centerboard trunk. Edges are apt to chip or break. To avoid any chipping and to ease the banging take a small piece of sponge rubber to which, on one side, some fast drying waterproof glue is applied. With the aid of a stick or long thin ruler, shove the sponge high up against the top of the inside of the centerboard trunk. Hold in position until the glue has a chance to set and hold. Now when the board has been violently raised the blow will be softened by the sponge.

THE CENTERBOARD TRUNK

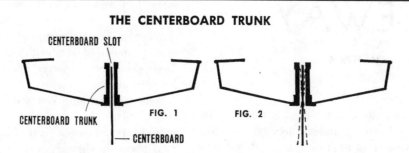

CENTERBOARD SLOT

CENTERBOARD TRUNK

FIG. 1

FIG. 2

CENTERBOARD

Fig. 1: when the centerboard slot is of proper width the centerboard will stay on true center. In Fig. 2, the dotted line indicates what happens when the centerboard slot is too wide. Besides shaking and twisting, the board falls away from true center and necessitates corrective helm.

A CENTERBOARD trunk must be strong in construction and of proper design not only to hold the centerboard, but to withstand racking side pressures. While the slot in the keel under the trunk should permit free raising or lowering of the board it should not be so wide that the board wobbles in the aperture and twists and allows water to build up inside the trunk. Turbulence disturbing the smooth flow of water under the hull slows the boat's progress. A wobbly board may become stuck in the trunk and it doesn't help speed at all. The cure for major centerboard trouble is a new trunk installed by a competent boatbuilder. Some one-design classes allow a rubber gasket to be placed on either side of the centerboard slot to stop any water from working up into the trunk. It is essential that the gasket be smoothly fitted. When the gasket wears out it must be replaced.

DAGGERBOARD VS THE CENTERBOARD

A DAGGERBOARD does a centerboard's work, but its shape and manner of operation are different. It provides stability, reduces leeway and aids steering. The accompanying drawing shows the relative shape and comparative position of the conventional centerboard and daggerboard. Because of one-design restrictions, some classes bar the daggerboard. In others it is required equipment.

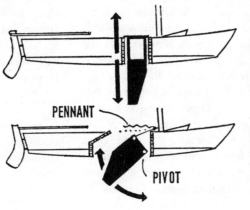

PENNANT

PIVOT

A daggerboard fully lowered. Arrows indicate the directional movement. A section is often cut out (white square), to reduce the weight of board.

A conventional centerboard half lowered. Arrows indicate the direction of movement to fully raised and fully lowered positions. Pivot corner and control pennant are shown.

THE CENTERBOARD

Moves forward when lowered and aft when raised. It pivots on a pin through its forward lower corner. Position is changed by hauling or releasing a pennant attached to the after upper corner, or forward upper corner. It is easy to handle.

Centerboards generally are rectangular in shape, longer than they are wide, but sometimes on large craft they take the form of a pie wedge.

The centerboard trunk extends into the cockpit, dividing it into two parts. The trunk needs strong construction as feet are braced against it and hiking straps and boom vangs often are attached to it.

Requires a larger opening in the keel than does a daggerboard, thereby creating greater underwater friction.

Should an underwater object be hit, normally the board will swing up out of harm's way.

Always housed or partly housed in its trunk except when all the way down.

As it is adjusted, there is greater spread in the fore and aft movement of the center of lateral resistance, thus necessitating sail trimming and changes in crew position.

THE DAGGERBOARD

Moves straight up and down, not on a pivot, by hand alone. It can be awkward to handle, particularly when the boat is heeled and strong side pressure is exerted.

Long and narrow in shape and lighter in weight than centerboard as a rule. Sometimes some of the board is cut away.

The daggerboard trunk is placed well forward, thereby allowing more room for movement in the cockpit. It is easier to brace when it is tied in with the foredeck.

Allows for a smaller opening in the keel, thereby reducing the underwater friction as compared to centerboard.

If an underwater object is hit the craft may come to a jarring halt and the board may be damaged severely.

When lowered, it is exposed below water as much as is a regular centerboard but when raised it extends upward to just below the boom and gets in the way of the sheets and boom vang.

The center of lateral resistance moves in a narrower range, because the board goes only one way—straight down.

LEEWAY

CHAPTER 9

Closely allied with centerboard control as discussed in the chapter previous is the matter of leeway, the side slip of a craft resulting from the action of wind and sea. It can best be explained by examining the diagram below which shows the relation between a course steered and a course sailed. The angular difference between the two is leeway.

Leeway can occur on any point of sailing except before the wind, but is most evident where side pressure is greatest.

To see how effective and important the centerboard is in reducing leeway, try to sail a predetermined course when there is a steady, moderate breeze.

The course should not be long, as both starting marker and finish point must be kept under continual observation. Set a course to windward or on a close reach. When the start is made, see that the centerboard is all the way down. Observe whether or not the craft is holding her course by constantly checking the alignment of the start and finish markers with the centerline of your boat. Note whether she holds up well or slides off some, information which can be useful when racing. The difference between the course you steer and the course you are making good is leeway, in this case with the centerboard down. Generally there is very little or none perceptible over a short course.

When halfway to the finish marker *raise* the centerboard all the way. The amount of leeway and increased angle of heel may surprise you. Complete the course and notice how far below the finish marker the boat comes. This should make you aware of how important centerboard control can be.

When sailing in strong wind and sea, leeway is much more pronounced, even with the centerboard fully lowered. These conditions, however, affect any craft, whether centerboard or keel.

When sailing long courses leeway may not be readily noticed. There are several ways to check. Because most small boats sail within sight of land, a marker on land such as a tower or chimney, or a buoy on the water, can be picked as a point to steer by. If, without a windshift, sheets must be constantly hauled for the craft to hold that point, then leeway exists or there is a set from current.

Two fixed objects in line ahead can be used as a range to detect leeway. If, while holding course, they stay in line, there is no leeway. If the range opens and one object bears to the right or left of the other (assuming no current or windshift), the boat is making leeway.

Another way of checking whether or not you are making leeway is to watch your wake while steering a constant heading. If it leaves dead astern (with only slight disturbances caused by wind and wave) there is no leeway. If it leaves at an angle to the keel, as shown in the sketch, that is the angle of leeway. The angle should be small, so it is difficult to observe. A crew member forward, sighting aft at a light line trailing astern, can best observe it. Not being dependent upon fixed objects, this method will work in the presence of current, which may offset or increase leeway as observed relative to the bottom.

In the examples above we assume that the problem is not complicated by drift, caused by current, which might offset or increase leeway.

LEEBOARDS

Sailing canoes and some dinghies use leeboards, a device similar in principle to a centerboard. They reduce leeway, and stiffen a craft to prevent excessive heel. As the photograph shows, a board is placed on one or both sides of the boat. These are bolted to a bar that runs athwartship. The bolts are tightened enough to hold the boards against water pressure, but loose enough so that the boards can be raised or lowered by a strong hand, pushing or pulling on a hand grip. Just as centerboard profile shape varies, so does that of leeboards. Some, with hand grips, are long and narrow; others are wide and elliptical with all underwater edges streamlined.

LEE HELM and WEATHER HELM

CHAPTER 10

WHEN a moving boat with correctly trimmed sails maintains a straight course in a fair wind (not a strong wind) with the tiller held easy on dead center, and the boat neither heads up into the wind nor falls away from the wind on its own accord, it is said to be *in balance*. Any disturbance of this balance is noticed in the movement of the helm.

Should the bow of the boat have a tendency to head up into the wind so that the tiller has to be held toward the windward or weather side for straight course steering, it is said that the craft has a *weather helm*.

Should the opposite happen—i.e., the bow falls away from the wind, to leeward, and the tiller has to be held to leeward of center for straight course steering—it is said that the craft has a *lee helm*.

Sailing with a *lee* or *weather* helm (when the craft sails off course with the tiller on center) is an indication that the craft is in *imbalance*.

Boats with either an extreme weather or lee helm sail an erratic course or lose speed.

They are slowed because the rudder, when moved from its straight, streamlined position abaft the hull, begins to act as a retarding factor. It produces rudder drag.

Extreme helm also produces a drag on the skipper. Constant moving of the tiller back and forth, fighting to keep a boat on a straight course, is tiring. However, fatigue can be overcome by exchanging positions with a crew member as often as is necessary.

A temporary weather helm can exist in strong winds or when the boat is heeled way over. The helm corrects when the wind lets up.

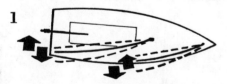

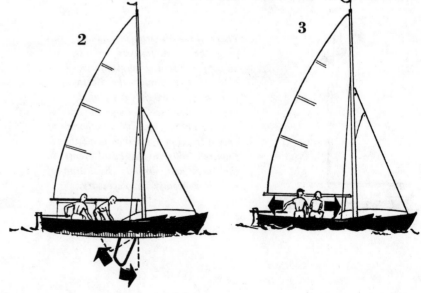

Each of these three illustrations show how adverse helm can be cured when sailing. Sometimes only one change is necessary, other times a combination of all three is needed before any improvement is noticed. (1) Adjusting sails, both jib and mainsail, (2) raising or lowering the centerboard, or (3) moving the crew forward or aft, are three of many measures that can be applied to correct for either weather or lee helm.

TEMPORARY CORRECTIONS WHEN UNDER WAY

TO CORRECT WEATHER HELM

Shift the crew aft—Often only a few inches are needed; other times a decided shift is called for. This raises the bow and causes the stern to grip the water more thoroughly.

Sail the boat with less heel—By moving the crew as far to windward as possible or by keeping a flutter in the sail, thereby sailing the boat as close to its designed waterline as possible.

Shift the movable heavy weights aft—Like anchors, anchor chain or ice chest. This causes the bow to raise. On cruising craft the imbalance of stowage can be quite an adverse factor.

Raise the centerboard—Until an effect is noticed on the helm.

Ease the main sheet—Thereby reducing side pressure on the mainsail.

Haul on the jib sheet—This increases side pressure on the sail, OR do both of the above.

TO CORRECT LEE HELM

Shift the crew forward—As far as is needed; this lowers the bow, causing it to grip deeper in the water, and raises the stern.

Sail the boat with more heel—This increases its waterline length, causing more of the hull to grip the water.

Shift the movable heavy weights forward—This causes the bow to dip.

Lower the centerboard—Until pressure is off the tiller.

Haul in on the main sheet—This increases its side pressure.

Slack the jib sheet—This relieves side pressure on the sail, OR do both of the above.

PERMANENT CORRECTIVE MEASURES

Of the listings below any one or several in combination can be effective

TO CORRECT WEATHER HELM

Decrease the rake in the mast—Tip the mast forward to a more upright position, keeping the heel in the same position. Stays and shrouds must also be readjusted.

Step the mast forward—Entire mast moves forward. The stays and shrouds must also be readjusted.

Raise the centerboard pivot pin—This reduces the amount of centerboard below the hull.

Move the centerboard pin aft—This moves a pressure factor aft.

Move the jibstay forward—Allows for larger fore triangle.

Increase the size of the jib—This also allows for a larger fore triangle, particularly on those craft that cannot move the forestay.

Decrease the size of the mainsail—This must be carefully done and done only after other methods have proved ineffective. A sailmaker should be consulted before any cutting is done.

Use a flatter mainsail—This decreases pressure.

Soften a tight leech—Any leech that is not straight but has a tendency to curl to windward can cause quite an imbalance. This can be easily cured by stretching the leech.

TO CORRECT LEE HELM

Increase the rake of the mast—Keep heel of mast in same position—tip the mast aft—means readjusting of stays and shrouds.

Step the mast aft—Entire mast moves aft—stays and shrouds must also be readjusted.

Lower the centerboard pivot pin—Increases the amount of board below the hull.

Move the centerboard pin forward—Moves a pressure factor forward.

Move the jibstay aft—Reduces the pressures forward.

Reduce the size of the jib—This also reduces the pressures forward but means recutting the sail.

Increase the size of the mainsail—Means getting a new sail.

Use a fuller mainsail—One with more draft or belly; generally means resewing by a sailmaker.

These three diagrams show (4) tipping the mast forward or aft, (5) moving the entire mast forward or aft, and (6) moving the jibstay forward or aft—are the easier of the permanent corrective methods for cure of adverse helm. Sometimes a change of only a fraction of an inch is all that is required plus slight adjustments in the stays and shrouds. Recutting of sails is generally not necessary.

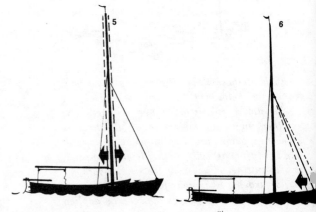

LEE HELM

Any degree of lee helm is considered bad because 1) should the helm be left unattended the craft will sail way off the wind and go into a series of jibes or knockdowns on unpredictable courses. 2) When beating, the craft will always have a tendency to sail away from its best point on the wind, causing the helmsman to constantly "fight the boat." 3) Should a skipper, sailing single-handed, fall overboard he has no chance of getting back on board because the craft will sail away. 4) Where constant luffing is necessary, to parry strong puffs of wind, a lee helm becomes an extra hazard because the boat has a tendency to bear off or may capsize.

A decided lee helm is to be avoided and should be immediately corrected. Such a condition invites trouble. If struck by a sudden puff or squall the boat could fail to come up into the wind on its own, despite corrective efforts by the helmsman.

WEATHER HELM

Some skippers consider a small degree of weather helm good because the craft will then have a tendency to head up toward its best point when beating. Where there is considerable weather helm, the craft will have a tendency to head up into the wind and stall or slow down.

Scientific tank testing on hulls has proved that any rudder held more than 2° from center produces rudder drag. Most racing skippers prefer the tiller and rudder to be always on center and so avoid this slowing action.

There is also a safety factor involved with a slight weather helm. When leaving the helm to lower sail during a squall, or for any reason where the tiller must be left unattended, the craft on its own accord will come up into the wind and stop. Should one fall overboard there is a good chance of swimming to and catching the craft.

HOW TO CORRECT LEE AND WEATHER HELM

In all instances the correction for lee helm and weather helm are opposite to one another. The size of the boat is an important factor as to the degree of corrective action needed. On a small, light, sensitive craft, subtle, easy changes may be all that is necessary. The slightest change may be effective. On large, heavy keel boats, decidedly greater changes may be necessary before a correction is noticed.

CE—CENTER OF EFFORT
CLR—CENTER OF LATERAL RESISTANCE

CE or Center of Effort is the point where wind forces are centered in the sails.

CLR or Center of Lateral Resistance is the point on the hull where the forces directed to the side of the hull are centered.

These points are not fixed or stationary but keep moving. Their movements depend on the position of the sails, strength of the wind, force of waves, and direction of sailing.

When the CE and CLR are in a theoretical line, working in harmony, a craft is in balance.

When the CE is forward of the CLR a craft will have a lee helm. There is a turning moment away from the wind. When the CE is aft of the CLR a craft will have a weather helm. There is a turning moment toward the wind. The further the CE and CLR are apart the greater the helm and stronger the turning moment.

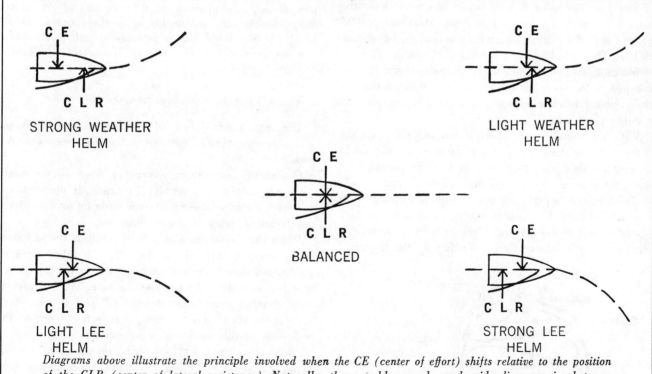

Diagrams above illustrate the principle involved when the CE (center of effort) shifts relative to the position of the CLR (center of lateral resistance). Naturally, there could never be such wide discrepancies between the two points in practice. For purposes of illustration, the differences have been greatly exaggerated. As CE shifts further aft, the stronger the weather helm. As CE moves forward, ahead of the CLR, we get lee helm. The center illustration shows a theoretically balanced condition.

BENDING and RAISING the MAINSAIL

To bend a sail is to make it fast to its proper spar, or stay, ready for setting

CHAPTER 11

Step by step procedure

THERE are a number of things that must be done before a sail can be raised. First, the rudder and tiller, if they are of the removable type, must be rigged. If they are permanently installed, tiller lashings should be removed so that the rudder can swing freely. Second, the mainsheet should be uncleated and made clear for running. (Do not remove the boom crotch until the sail is two-blocked aloft.) Third, release the main halyard and its shackle from the outhaul, where it was secured after the previous sail, and snap it temporarily somewhere near the mast.

After the above has been attended to, and not before, the sail is taken out of its bag. Attaching a sail to the spars is called "bending on sail." Take hold of the foot of the sail at its clew corner and straighten any kinks or twists by running the hand along the foot rope. This lines up the slides and makes them easier to handle.

Slip the first slide at the clew end onto the boom track at the mast. Pull the clew out, inserting the other slides in order, until the clew is almost to the end of the boom.

Release the outhaul line, push the outhaul to the clew and fasten together. Go to the mast end of the boom and fasten the tack of the sail to the gooseneck. Now back to the clew end to haul the outhaul hand taut.

Now take the halyard, hold it out and away from the mast. Look aloft to see if it is clear. If it has twisted around any of the stays, shrouds or spreaders, be sure to clear it. Then shackle it to the head of the mainsail.

With the sail hanging loosely by the halyard and its foot fastened to the boom, insert the battens. Be sure they fit their respective batten pockets and are tied in securely with a tight square knot.

With one hand slowly raising the halyard, slip the slides sewn on the luff rope onto the mast track. Should a crew member be handy, he can haul on the halyard while the skipper slips the sail slides onto the mast track.

Raise the sail as high as it can go without binding in the masthead sheave. For proper setting of a sail, all slack should be out of the halyard. Slack in the halyard can be eliminated by what is called "sweating up the halyard."

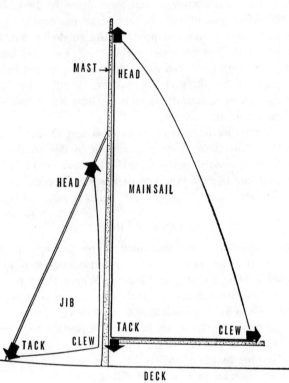

Mast and boom fittings must be so placed that there is a straight-line, direct pull to all three corners of the mainsail; otherwise, the sail works out of shape and wrinkles form. The jib should have a straight-line pull at the tack and at the head, so that the luff is straight and hard.

This will remove all scallops from the sail.

The main halyard can be stretched in three different ways, all depending on the type of boom gooseneck on the mast.

Goosenecks come three ways: (1) fixed on the mast; cannot be raised or lowered; (2) can slide up or down, 4″ to 6″, on a metal rod; (3) can slide up or down on a mast track, as much as two or three feet.

When the gooseneck is at a fixed position, the sail must be "sweated up" to stretch the luff. The other types of goosenecks permit the sail to be raised to the top of the mast, or as high as the gooseneck allows. The luff rope is then stretched by a "boom downhaul." This is a line fastened at the mast, near the deck; it runs to a block on the underside of the gooseneck, then down to a cleat, either on deck or on the mast. By heaving on the downhaul, the boom is lowered, and this automatically takes up any slack in the hoist.

Many racing classes have black bands painted around the mast alow and aloft. They indicate (because of racing class rules) that the boom cannot be lowered beyond the mark (nor the head of the sail above the upper band).

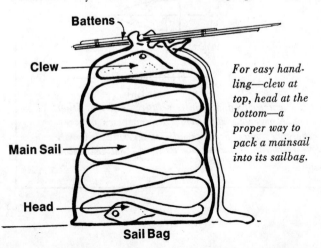

Battens

Clew

Main Sail

Head

Sail Bag

For easy handling—clew at top, head at the bottom—a proper way to pack a mainsail into its sailbag.

30

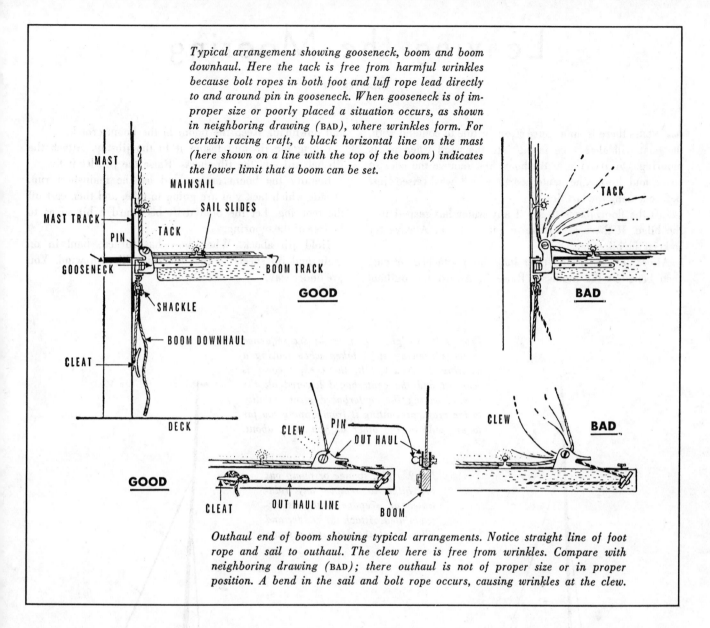

Typical arrangement showing gooseneck, boom and boom downhaul. Here the tack is free from harmful wrinkles because bolt ropes in both foot and luff rope lead directly to and around pin in gooseneck. When gooseneck is of improper size or poorly placed a situation occurs, as shown in neighboring drawing (BAD), where wrinkles form. For certain racing craft, a black horizontal line on the mast (here shown on a line with the top of the boom) indicates the lower limit that a boom can be set.

MAST

MAINSAIL

MAST TRACK — SAIL SLIDES

TACK

PIN

GOOSENECK — TACK — BOOM TRACK

GOOD

SHACKLE

BOOM DOWNHAUL

CLEAT

DECK

TACK

BAD

GOOD

CLEW — PIN — OUT HAUL

CLEAT — OUT HAUL LINE — BOOM

CLEW — **BAD**

Outhaul end of boom showing typical arrangements. Notice straight line of foot rope and sail to outhaul. The clew here is free from wrinkles. Compare with neighboring drawing (BAD); there outhaul is not of proper size or in proper position. A bend in the sail and bolt rope occurs, causing wrinkles at the clew.

Too much tension should never be put on a halyard; otherwise, the sail can stretch out of shape.

Should the slides jam or stick, the halyard should be slowly raised and lowered, moved up and down, to soften or wear down the burr or dirt that is hindering easy movement.

All slides on foot and luff of the sail must slip onto their respective tracks in proper order. These slides are evenly spaced and furnish an even grip on the tracks.

One of the greatest strains occurs at the outhaul. It must be strongly rigged and secured.

Normally, the main halyard leads down the starboard side of the mast and the jib halyard on the port side to cleats at the foot of the mast, on deck, or below deck.

The first sail to be raised on any boat, under ordinary conditions, is the one furthest aft. On a sloop, the mainsail is raised first; on a yawl or ketch, it is the mizzen; and on a two-masted schooner, it is the mainsail. Raising the aftmost sail helps to keep the craft headed into the wind. Should a jib or foresail be raised first, the boat is apt to sail around at its mooring, making it difficult to raise the other sails.

Leaving the Mooring

CHAPTER 12

Unless there is an adverse stronger tide to contend with, the boat will always be facing into the wind when at its mooring. On arriving at the boat, first remove the cockpit cover and lower the centerboard, which was raised just before leaving the last time.

Lift the floorboards to see if any water has seeped into the bilge. If there is, sponge or pump it out. Always try to keep the bilge dry.

After the rudder and tiller have been attached, unbag, then bend on the mainsail. Raise it. Adjust the outhaul and downhaul. Keep the boom in the boom crotch.

Unbag the jib and fasten it to the jibstay. Attach the jib halyard and the jib sheets. Raise the jib, let it fly.

Remove the boom crotch and let the mainsheet run. Decide which tack you are going to take, and then cast off the mooring. Let the boat drift backward a bit so as to be free of the mooring.

Hold jib aback. When bow has turned, haul in on main and jib sheets so that the sails fill with wind. You are under way.

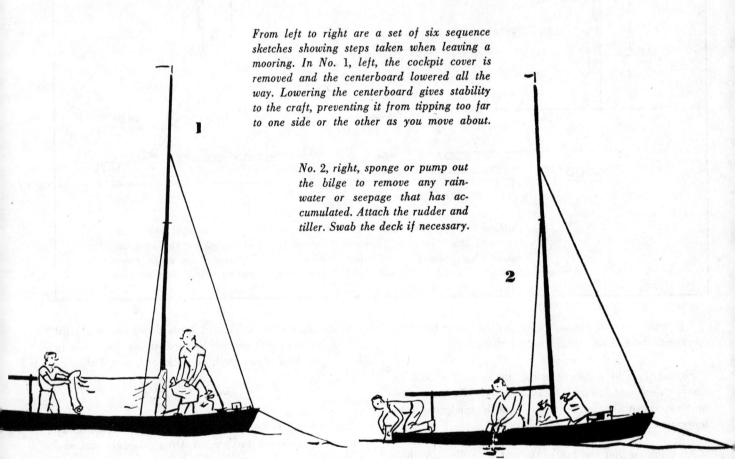

From left to right are a set of six sequence sketches showing steps taken when leaving a mooring. In No. 1, left, the cockpit cover is removed and the centerboard lowered all the way. Lowering the centerboard gives stability to the craft, preventing it from tipping too far to one side or the other as you move about.

No. 2, right, sponge or pump out the bilge to remove any rainwater or seepage that has accumulated. Attach the rudder and tiller. Swab the deck if necessary.

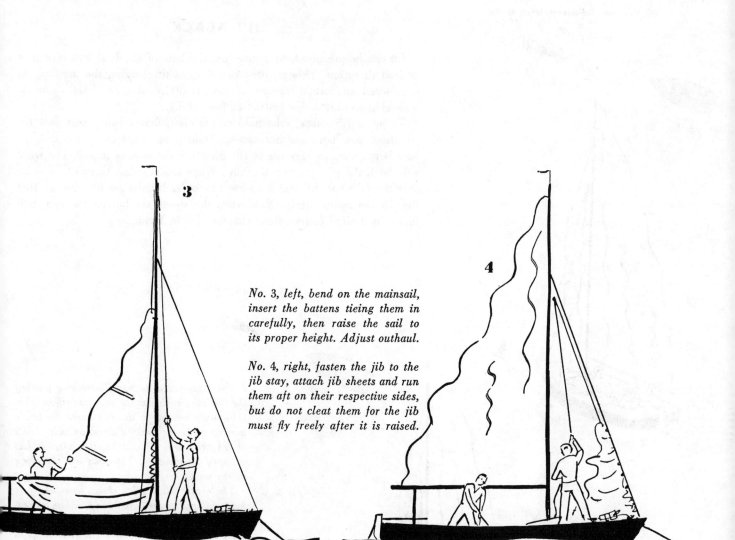

No. 3, left, bend on the mainsail, insert the battens tieing them in carefully, then raise the sail to its proper height. Adjust outhaul.

No. 4, right, fasten the jib to the jib stay, attach jib sheets and run them aft on their respective sides, but do not cleat them for the jib must fly freely after it is raised.

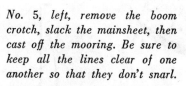

No. 5, left, remove the boom crotch, slack the mainsheet, then cast off the mooring. Be sure to keep all the lines clear of one another so that they don't snarl.

No. 6, right, hold the jib aback (see illustrations on following page) then when the bow has turned, haul in on main and jib sheets. To get good movement on the boat sail away on a reach.

"W" with arrow indicates direction of wind.

JIB ABACK

JIB can be put aback to assure that the bow of the boat will turn in a desired direction. This is often necessary when leaving the mooring in a crowded anchorage because of the proximity of other boats, a dock, a shoal or an obstruction restricting free sailing.

To put a jib aback, take hold of the clew, first making sure that the jib sheets are loose and not cleated. Hold it out opposite to the side the bow is to swing or opposite to the direction the boat is to sail. The wind will catch the jib and turn the bow. When the bow has turned to a point that the sails can fill and a course can be sailed, let go the clew so that the jib can swing freely. Now when the sheets are hauled the boat will be on its desired course. Read chapter 15—In Irons.

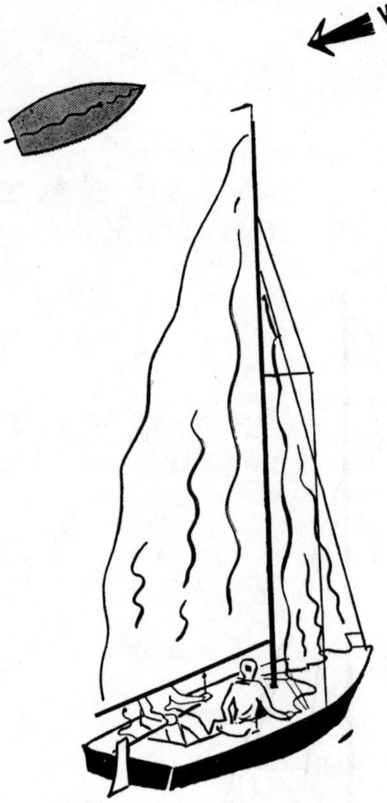

Three sequence drawings illustrating putting the jib aback—a simple easy maneuver that takes only seconds to do. It assures the bow's turning off in the desired direction. Above left shows the craft, all sail hoisted, after it has dropped its mooring. The sails are fluttering in the wind.

The center illustration shows how the jib is held out (put aback) until the bow has turned.

The illustration below shows the boat, all sails trimmed, sailing off on a clear course.

CURRENT ➡️

◀️ WIND

LEAVING THE MOORING—
WIND AND TIDE
FROM DIFFERENT DIRECTIONS
AND TIDE STRONGER THAN WIND

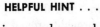

CURRENT ➡️   ◀️ W

IN a situation of this kind first bend on the jib, then bend the mainsail to mast and boom, but do not raise it. It is very difficult to raise and control the mainsail when at the mooring without its swinging the boat around in wild gyrations. Continue to hold the boom in the boom crotch. Raise the jib, make fast the jib halyard.

Uncleat and drop the mooring, haul on jib sheet so that the sail fills. Sail down-wind under jib alone. When you have enough way on the boat and are also clear of other boats and obstructions, swing around into the wind. Quickly raise the mainsail. Remember the boat will drift some, and the wind may turn you, so allow enough sea room. Put the jib aback so the bow falls off. Now, with all the sail up, sail on a reach to again pick up momentum.

◀️ W

HELPFUL HINT . . .

A good skipper and crew check as they leave the mooring. How are the sails set-tight? Are the sheets set right for the wind and course sailed? Is the wind pennant swinging properly? Is the boat responding to movements of the tiller? Anything ahead of us?

This diagram illustrates the normal maneuver in getting underway from a mooring. First, drifting to clear the mooring, then putting the jib aback to turn the bow in the direction to be sailed. Second, hauling on the sheets to adjust sails for a reach. The boat thereby gathers good momentum. Third, again adjusting sails for the course.

Coming About

*Coming about is the maneuver of changing from one tack to
the other, the bow swinging through the eye of the wind*

CHAPTER 13

THE maneuver of coming about is easy to execute. Merely
steer the boat towards the eye of the wind and continue
around until the sails fill on the other side, executing a
90° turn. The forward momentum carries the boat around
to its new course.

To illustrate, suppose you are sailing close-hauled. The
helmsman gives the command, "Ready about." This warns
the crew that the boat will come about and alerts them to
be ready to handle sheets and move to the opposite side
of the craft.

The command of execution is "hard a lee." The helmsman moves the tiller over to leeward (away from the
wind). The bow swings into the wind and as the jib starts
to flutter, the sheet is let go. The sails luff, then swing to
the other side of the boat. The mainsail again fills with
wind as does the jib, but the jib sheet, being loose, is
hauled in to trim the sail. The crew moves inboard and
continues moving across the boat as the boat turns and the
sails fill with wind on the other tack. The tiller is put
amidships (on center) and the boat steered to its course.
The boat has been put about and is now sailing on the
other tack.

Letting the jib sheet loose takes the pressure of wind
from the bow, allowing the boat to swing more easily. The
jib sheet should be loosened only after the jib starts to
flutter, which is but a moment or two after the tiller is
moved. Useful drive in the sail is thus maintained until
no longer needed.

The mainsail is held fast in position, not touched or
adjusted.

On many racing boats only one command is given when
coming about. The skipper after giving the command
"Ready about" waits a few seconds, then pushes the tiller
over. The pause between the command and pushing the
tiller over gives the crew the few moments needed to prepare the lines for the quick maneuver. This can be done
because the crew is constantly on the alert. In ordinary
day sailing the skipper waits until all in the boat are ready
before giving the second part of the two-part command.

How a boat is trimmed may affect its turning movement.
If there is too much weight forward the bow may bury

itself excessively in the sea and hinder the coming about
procedure. If there's too much weight in the stern, causing
the bow to lift from the water, the wind may keep the bow
from turning.

If the craft fails to make the turn to come about and
refuses to answer the helm to head one way or the other
the craft is said to be "in irons."

To get out of irons hold the rudder in a position opposite to the direction you want to steer and also put the
jib aback to turn the bow toward the direction you want
to steer. Only when fully about, (not halfway or three-
quarters way for the craft may swing back) should the
tiller be set for the new course or the sheets trimmed and
set. (See chapter 15 for additional text and illustrations on
this subject.)

To avoid getting into irons keep good momentum on the
boat as it comes around. Sometimes the tiller has to be
snapped over and other times brought around easy with a
long shoot into the wind. The latter in good sailing
breezes, the former in light airs.

If the wind is so light that the craft cannot come around
on its own momentum it may need some coaxing. The
sheets should be slackened and a bit of sculling resorted
to (though not when racing). Sculling is moving the tiller
back and forth. It gives some slight forward movement to
the boat. In ordinary sailing breezes no trouble should be
encountered.

When coming about in strong wind and big seas a boat
quickly loses way. Its turning movement is stopped somewhat by the force of the waves. Keep good way on the craft
and wait for the smoother, smaller rollers to come along.

In squally weather it is best not to come about in the
strong puffs of wind as the sails shake excessively, and
forward movement may be stopped. Wait until the puff
has passed.

Generally a boat should come about easily with good
momentum so that it can shoot up into the wind a bit before turning.

The tiller should never be slammed over to an extreme
turning angle as the rudder may then act as a brake and
stop the boat's forward movement.

LUFFING—*The term luffing is taken from that part of the sail that first starts to shiver and shake when steering the boat too close to the wind.*

When heading directly into the wind and the sails shake or flutter you are luffing.

If the boat is being steered too close to the direction of wind and the luff of the sails start to shiver you are starting to luff.

You are said to luff up when you deliberately steer the boat toward the eye of the wind.

WIND

The diagram illustrates the turning movement of a craft when coming about.

How the JIBE differs from COMING ABOUT

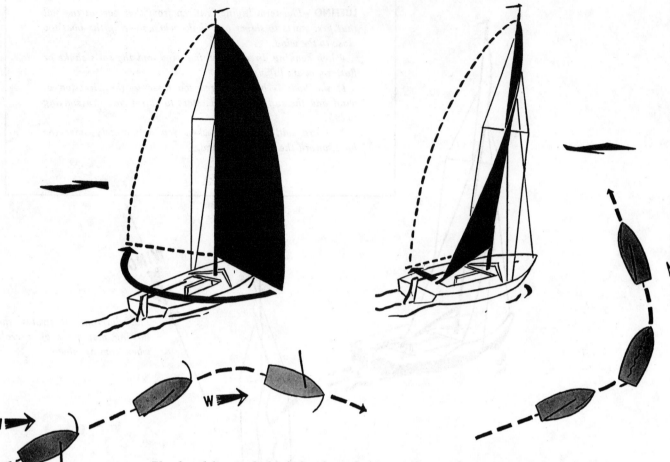

The dotted line in both of the above drawings indicates the position of the sails after the maneuver has been accomplished. The "W" with arrow indicates wind direction.

THE JIBE

IN THE jibe the wind is from aft. The stern of the boat and the leech of the sail pass through the eye of the wind in going from one tack to the other. The difference in the courses of the tacks may vary from zero degrees to 180 degrees, depending on the course to be sailed.

COMING ABOUT

IN COMING about, the wind is from ahead. The bow and the luff of the sails pass through the eye of the wind as the boat goes from one tack to the other. Generally the tacks are no closer than 90° from each other or 45° from the direction of the wind.

A boat turns on its
CENTER OF ROTATION

A BOAT turns on its center of rotation. It does not turn like an automobile where the rear wheels almost follow in line with the front wheels when turning.

A boat's bow turns in the direction you want it to go *but* the stern swings the other way. There is a sliding or skidding effect.

This action is of concern when you are (1) sailing very close to another boat, (2) rounding a buoy, or (3) turning into a marina.

In close quarters the skipper must watch the stern as it swings, as well as the bow. Enough room should always be allowed for the stern to swing without its hitting another boat, a buoy or a stake.

On a small centerboard boat the center of rotation is about where the centerboard is, so the bow and stern will swing almost equally. On a keel boat, where much of the deep keel is aft, the center of rotation will be further aft. This means that the bow will swing more than the stern when the boat is turning.

The illustration at the left is comparable to a set of sequence photos. All three Atlantic class boats are in different phases of rounding a marker, the flag of which shows. The boat at the left has come about and is sailing off on the port tack. The center boat is turning to come about and is in the middle of its luff. The boat at the right is on the starboard tack just before the turn to come about. (Morris Rosenfeld photo)

HAND OVER HAND—A term used when hauling in on the main sheet and all parts of the sheets are handed at one time, one hand after and over the other. This is often practiced when the wind is light or when jibing and there is practically no strain on the sheets. It is an easy, quick way to haul. It saves excess pulling, particularly when the boom is far out, as when running.

TAPING TURNBUCKLES
Taping turnbuckles prevents the sails from catching on cotter pins and tearing, and reduces chafing of sails and sheets.

Tacking

Tacking is beating to windward on alternate courses

CHAPTER 14

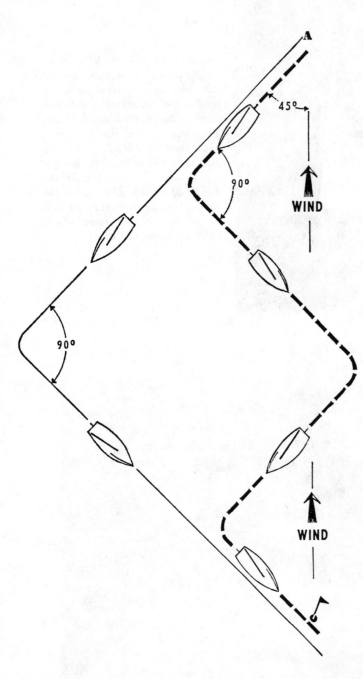

Aboat cannot be sailed in the exact direction from which the wind comes. But to get to a point or marker upwind, a boat can sail a zig-zag course. Each zig or zag is sailed as close to the wind direction as possible (approximately 45° to the true wind or 90° from the previous course or tack). You sail close hauled first on one tack, come about, then sail on the other tack, come about, and repeat until the destination is reached.

Short hitches or tacks can be taken, represented by the heavy dotted line in the accompanying diagram, or long hitches or tacks can be sailed, represented by the thin line. However, in ordinary day sailing when the wind is coming directly from the point to be reached, if tacks taken are long, the marker may be lost sight of and you may sail far above it. So it is wiser, more often than not, to take shorter tacks.

There are times when you will reach your destination faster by taking a series of long tacks along with short tacks. Such occasions arise when the wind is coming from a sector to the left or the right of a marker (other than directly from it). If the wind is coming from the right or to starboard of the marker the long tack will be a starboard tack (in which the wind comes over the starboard bow). The opposite is true when the wind is coming from the left or port side of the marker. Here the long tack will be the port tack. In both instances the long tack will always bring the craft closer to its destination.

When on the last tack and you wish to gauge the right point to come about and "lay a marker," measure the 90° angle. You face forward in your boat and extend your arm out sideways on the side the marker is on. By sighting along your extended arm you will see when your hand points directly at the marker that that is the time to come about for it is 90° to your present course. If your craft cannot tack in 90°, greater allowance must be made. By gauging the greater angle from the bow, the point to come about is determined.

Should you overstand the marker on the last tack, it is easy to sail off or down to it. But should you estimate that you are sailing short of the marker it is better to continue on the same course until you are at the point where by coming about (using the above method) you will lay the marker.

In boating language a short tack is called "a short board" and a long tack "a long board."

WHEN under way a boat is always on a tack, regardless of whether it is beating, reaching or running. If the wind comes over the port side it is on a port tack, and if it comes over the starboard side it is on a starboard tack. But the maneuver of beating on alternate courses is called tacking.

This diagram illustrates the difference between short tacks and a long tack; short tacks indicated by the heavy dotted line and a long tack by the solid thin line. The difference is that you come about more often on the short tacks to reach a marker or destination. Long tacks are most always preferred, as a steady maximum speed can be maintained. Short tacks slow the boat, demand constant adjusting of sails, and also cause the crew to constantly shift from side to side. However, short tacks are necessary when following a channel, sailing through a mooring area, adjusting to wind shifts, and where the tactical situation so dictates in racing.

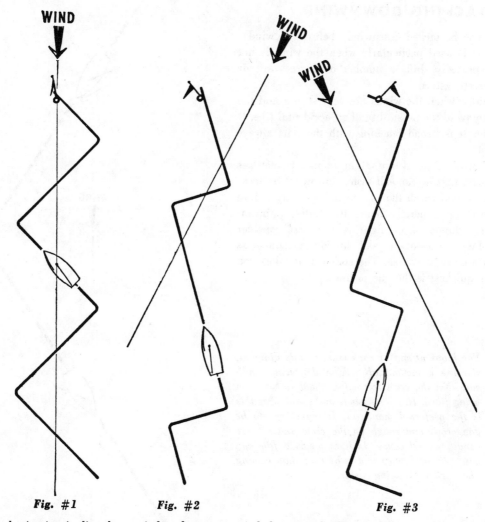

WIND

WIND

WIND

Fig. #1   **Fig. #2**   **Fig. #3**

When the marker or destination is directly to windward, corresponding tacks to reach this point are of equal lengths as indicated in Fig. #1. When the marker is not directly to windward but to the port or starboard of the true wind direction the tacks then become unequal in length; one tack becomes longer than the other. The further the marker is away from the true wind direction the longer the long tack becomes. The short tack then becomes correspondingly shorter. The ultimate is reached where the marker is fetched in one long tack. When the wind is from starboard of the marker, the long tack is a starboard tack as shown in Fig. #2. When the wind is from the port of the marker the long tack is a port tack (Fig. #3).

Class boats tacking to a mark. When to tack, or gauging the right distance to the mark, is most important when racing. Sailing a longer course than necessary may be detrimental to winning or fishing with leaders of the fleet.

TACKING DOWNWIND

A BOAT can also be tacked downwind (before the wind). This maneuver is used particularly when the wind is not steady but repeatedly shifts a number of degrees left or right from directly astern.

It is also done when the winds are very strong and the waves high, to avoid the possibility of an accidental jibe. It is safe sailing. It is broad reaching with the sails always under control.

Tacking downwind is also used in racing. Sometimes a skipper figures that he can sail faster downwind by tacking on a very broad reach than by sailing directly before the wind, reaching generally being the fastest point of sailing. But the skipper in his figuring must also consider the extra distance necessary to sail this zig-zag course as compared to a straight course. The course that takes you to your mark quickest is the one to use.

WIND

The loops at end of each tack, in this diagram, showing a method of tacking downwind, indicate that the craft is coming about rather than being jibed. In strong winds and rough seas this is the preferred maneuver. Jibing is apt to be dangerous and rough on the crew under these conditions. Of course in light winds a jibe can easily be performed and is quicker than coming about when changing course.

WIND

HELPFUL HINT . . .

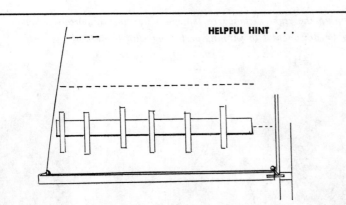

PATCHING SAILS WITH ADHESIVE TAPE

Keep on hand a roll of wide adhesive tape (minimum width 2"), for it is most useful in patching sails should they ever tear and need immediate repair. The illustration indicates how a long wide piece follows the length of the tear. This in turn is reinforced by shorter narrower cross pieces. It is an effective temporary measure. It prevents tearing or further destruction until the sail can be repaired by the sailmaker.

IN IRONS

ALSO CALLED "CAUGHT IN STAYS"

A boat is said to be "in irons" when she is headed directly into the wind, is motionless or drifting astern, the sails shaking, and she cannot come around on either tack. Getting in irons generally is caused by coming about too slowly, the boat's momentum being insufficient to carry the bow through the eye of the wind.

CHAPTER 15

DIFFERENT types of boats require slightly different methods to get out of "irons." The bow on some boats must be made to turn; on others the stern. Some boats require that both bow and stern be swung in order to get out of this condition and have the sails again fill. Several such methods are presented here.

The position of the tiller does not matter when the boat is stationary in the water. If the craft has sternway, shift the tiller to the side you want the bow to swing. When sails fill and the boat has headway, steer a normal course.

The small, fast, popular centerboarders are easily maneuvered out of this sail-slatting, halting predicament. Because of their wonderful sail balance, a few quick jerks of the tiller (to move the stern around) usually suffices to get the sails to fill again.

Sometimes, however, this may not be sufficient. Then the jib should be quickly backed opposite to the direction the bow is to turn. The main is allowed to swing freely. This action should turn any lively craft, enough for the sails to draw again. It takes only a few seconds. Raising the centerboard in conjunction with backing the jib will help but often is unnecessary.

Should the boat be of a more sluggish type or have a long keel, the additional action of moving the rudder opposite to the direction the craft is to turn will help. But the resulting braking and turning action becomes effective only after the craft has developed sternway.

Methods used in getting out of "irons" are also used when leaving a mooring to bring a boat's heading to a desired tack. Any craft, when under mainsail alone, about to leave the mooring, but still fast to it, can be turned by backing the mainsail. This swings the stern. The sail must be held aback for a longer time than a jib ordinarily would be, as it takes longer for the stern to swing. It also takes more beef to hold the mainsail out on a large boat. If the wind is strong it may require the efforts of three or four men.

For this method to be effective, hauling in of the mainsheet when the craft has swung to its proper angle (more than 45°) to the wind must be coordinated with the quick release of the mooring. A most seamanlike impression is created when this maneuver is performed properly.

IN IRONS

HOW TO GET OUT OF IRONS

1. If your boat has sternway, push the tiller over in the direction you want the bow to swing. 2. Hold the jib aback, on the side opposite the tiller, so it catches the wind and turns the bow. This turning movement can be helped by sculling (quickly moving the tiller back and forth).

The simplest way to get out of irons, though painfully slow, is for the skipper to release all sheets and to pull up the centerboard. He sits and waits until the craft slowly swings broadside to the wind. (It may go to port or starboard; there is no control of direction.) Only then are the sheets trimmed for the sails to fill. The jib is adjusted first, for this prevents the bow from turning into the wind, which may happen if the main sheet is taken in first.

THREE METHODS
FOR GETTING OUT OF IRONS
WITH
A SAILING DINGHY

SAILING dinghies are handled differently. There are three methods used to get a sailing dinghy out of irons (turning momentum is created by different handling of the sail). In method 1, its boom and tiller are pushed in the direction the craft is to turn. The boom is pushed out by hand only so far as to allow the after end of the sail to catch wind; the luff should shake. The tiller is pushed over as far as it will go.

The wind will catch and push against the after part of the sail and cause the stern to swing. A quick, sharp reversal of the tiller will aid this movement. The boom is then let go. As the craft comes around the sheet is trimmed and the craft put on its predetermined course. Sculling or perhaps a few rapid jerks on the tiller to impart a slight forward and turning movement, helps when the boom is thus held out. Sculling is not allowed when racing but can be used at any other time.

In the second method the boom is also pushed out by hand but opposite to the direction the craft is to sail. At the same time the tiller is thrown to the side opposite to the boom, to aid in turning the stern while the boat has sternway. The boom is held out far enough to allow the whole sail to catch wind (45° to the true wind).

The boom is held out only long enough to swing the bow. As the boat approaches the desired heading the boom is then allowed to swing to leeward to the position it will take on the new tack, and the sheet trimmed accordingly.

When the third method is used, the mainsheet is slacked, the centerboard raised and the tiller pointed way over in the direction the craft is to head. The crew weight should be kept toward the stern so that the bow raises and the stern lowers in the water. As the boat gathers sternway the bow will be swung around by the wind. When the craft's heading is right for the course to be sailed, the centerboard is lowered and the sheets hauled for the sail to again catch wind.

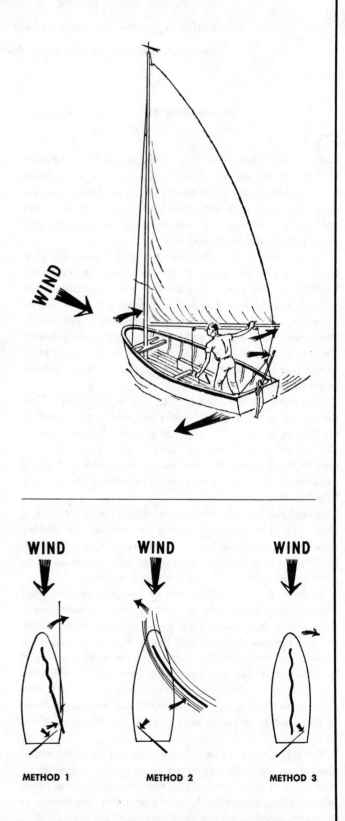

WIND

WIND   WIND   WIND

METHOD 1   **METHOD 2**   **METHOD 3**

TIGHT JIB SHEET METHOD OF GETTING OUT OF IRONS

In this method five things must be done before the boat will turn and the sails fill again.

1) The jib sheet, on the side opposite that to which the craft is to turn is hauled in tight and made fast. Fig. A.

2) The tiller is moved way over and should point in the direction toward which the craft is to turn. This puts the rudder on the same side of the boat as the tight jib sheet. Fig. B.

3) Skipper and crew must keep weight in center of boat or slightly on the tight jib side.

4) The mainsheet is allowed to run free.

5) The centerboard should be raised. The wind striking the jib creates both a turning and a pushing action. This pushing action creates sternway. The rudder then acts as a brake against sternway while the bow continues to swing.

When the bow has swung enough for the sails to fill, the jib sheet is let go and then made fast on the lee side as the wind carries the sail to leeward. A sharp jerk on the tiller also helps head the boat on her proper course, Fig. C. Only then is the mainsheet hauled and adjusted for this point of sailing. The centerboard should also be lowered, if necessary, for the course to be sailed. Fig. D.

WIND

This is not a quick method to bring a craft out of irons. However, it is handy, should you be sailing single-handed and not want to leave the tiller unattended. Much of the turning motion depends on the rudder acting as a brake on one side of the stern, as the craft develops sternway and the bow swings.

A   B   C   D

GETTING A YAWL OUT OF IRONS

A YAWL is often brought out of irons by backing the jigger or after sail. It can also be turned much faster by backing both the jigger and jib opposite to each other. The jigger turns the stern and the jib turns the bow as the boat swings on its center of rotation. The main sheet is not made fast but is allowed to run free until the craft has turned enough for the mainsail to fill. Both jib and jigger sheets are then released simultaneously and adjusted for the new tack.

In the diagram at the right the heavy arrows at bow and stern indicate how bow and stern will swing. Should the jigger not be put back but be sheeted tightly amidships, it would hinder any turning motion created by putting the jib aback, for it then acts as a wind vane and holds the bow into the wind. The jigger should be backed or its sheet released.

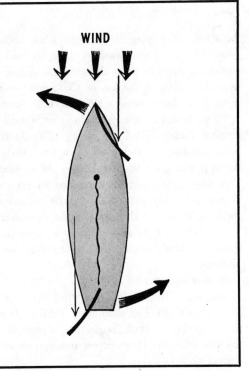

WIND

Jibing

*To jibe is to bring the boat around to
the other tack "stern" into the wind.*

CHAPTER 16

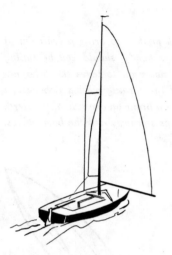

*Above are four sequence drawings
illustrating the jibe. In No. 1, above,
the boom and mainsail are far out to
starboard. The boat is running before the wind, centerboard dropped.*

*In step No. 2, the boom has been
hauled in to a tight close reach position. The wind is aft, still holding
the mainsail on the starboard side.*

*In step No. 3, the jib sheet is re-
leased, then the course is changed.
As the stern swings, the wind gets
behind the sail and the boom snaps
over to the opposite or port side as
in this instance. Sheets are never
fastened but held by hand. The crew
must be ready to shift positions,
dodge boom as it swings over, and
work the sheets. Drawing shows both
the mainsail and jib as they have
swung over and filled on opposite
side of boat.*

GENERALLY you use the jibe when sailing before the
wind, (1) when you want to change your course without
coming about, (2) when the wind has shifted and you want
to avoid sailing by the lee, or (3) when you have to round
a buoy or breakwater where there is limited sea room.

There is still another situation that is used in windward-
leeward racing called the racing jibe: At the end of the
beat, you have to swing off on a run (with the boom on
the opposite side) when rounding the weather mark.

A jibe should not be attempted in very strong winds.
When the going gets really rough, experienced skippers
sheet in, tack, and then ease to the new course.

However, in light and ordinary winds a jibe is a routine
maneuver easily performed but it should be controlled at
all time.

Here is how it is done.

You are sailing before the wind with the boom out as
far as it will go. For additional stability, if the craft is of
the centerboard type, begin the maneuver by dropping
the centerboard. Haul in on the mainsheet, maintaining
course while so doing.

Keep hauling on the mainsheet until it is almost as tight
as when you are beating. Release the jib sheet so that the
jib swings freely. Keep the mainsheet (the part you are
hauling in) clear so that it can run out freely and quickly
without snarling—That means let the coils of the sheet
drop loosely one over the other. *Don't* allow them to be
kicked around.

Steer carefully and slowly to the side the boom is on.
The wind will get in back of the mainsail and swing the
boom over. The boom will snap over fast. Keep your head
low, shift weight to opposite side, and don't get tangled in
the mainsheet. To ease the jolt let the mainsheet run out
but control its run out so that the boom will not bang the
shrouds. Push the tiller to center, adjust the jib sheet so
that the jib again draws, and you are on course again.

Some skippers, when jibing in very light air, haul in the
mainsheet "hand over hand." That is, instead of hauling
the sheets through the blocks, they gather or pull in the
sheet as if they were hauling and gathering in a line.
After the boom has passed over, they also let out the sheet,
now on the opposite side, "hand over hand."

In step No. 4, as the boom comes over, the mainsheet is slowly released until the sail is at its correct angle to the wind. Then the jib sheet is trimmed for proper setting of jib.

If, as at right, sheet is not shortened before jibe, boom may swing up and foul backstay.

REMEMBER TO ALWAYS SHORTEN SHEET BEFORE A JIBE. Always control its operation. Do not let the boom swing free from one side to the other except in the very, very lightest airs.

In the lightest of variable and shifting airs, where there is no strain on the mast or rigging, the boom is often pushed by hand from one side to the other. You will often see this done in races where the skippers are anxious to pick up the slightest of breezes to gain a few yards in distance.

It has been said that there are only two kinds of jibes, the controlled one and the accidental one. The controlled jibe you have just read about.

The accidental jibe can be dangerous and destructive. It can be caused by a sudden shift of wind or by a careless helmsman. Imagine the boom and sail swinging over rapidly without control. Your head may be in the way and you may get knocked overboard. The sheets may also foul the tiller or snarl into a knot, leaving you without control of your craft.

When the wind shifts or swings from one quarter to the other and a prescribed course is to be maintained, a jibe is in order. This avoids the hazardous and worrisome sailing "by the lee."

"W" with arrow indicates wind direction.

SWING OF WIND

47

In the very light variable airs, where the boat is barely moving, the boom is often pushed from one side to the other to quicken the jibe. This is often done when racing, where it is imperative to catch every small zephyr that will keep the boat moving ahead. Not much attention is paid to the handling of sheets as described in the text, except to keep from being entangled in them as they sweep across the cockpit.

With the wind steady from one direction, the course of a sailboat, while sailing before the wind, can be altered by jibing. This is often done when having to round a buoy off a point of land, then having to sail a different course that will bring the wind to the other quarter of the vessel. (Illustration above)

Timing, when jibing around and going between breakwaters, is of utmost importance. Because of the limited area, preparations for the jibe must be completed well in advance so when the jibe is executed there is plenty of sailing room on either beam for further maneuver, should the need arise.

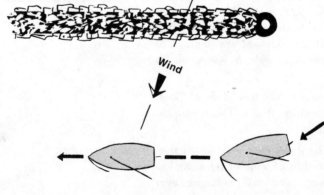

"W" with arrow indicates wind direction.

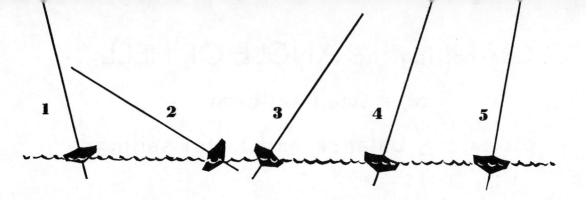

Above, bow views of the comparative angles of heel in the racing jibe, as depicted in the diagram below. It readily illustrates the critical point of this jibe, #2 and #3, where extreme caution and quick action are necessary.

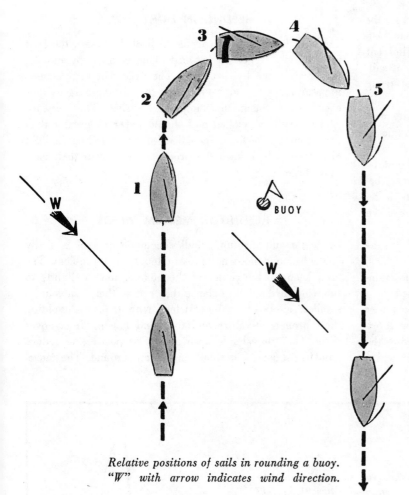

Relative positions of sails in rounding a buoy. "W" with arrow indicates wind direction.

THE RACING JIBE

IN both diagrams the numerals show comparative positions of the boat during the racing jibe. Numerals 1 show the normal close-hauled position and angle of heel of the craft approaching the buoy.

At numbers 2, the boom is hauled in as tight as it will come. From the diagrams it can be seen that the dangerous part of the jibe is when the sail is flat to the full force of the wind. In a strong wind a knockdown can occur here.

At numbers 3, the tiller is snapped over fast. As the wind forces the sail over, the crew must be ready and extremely nimble to shift weight from one high side to the other, as the boat makes an extremely sharp turn.

At numbers 4, the sheets are let out and at numbers 5, the sheets and sails are set for the run back.

In light winds this maneuver is accomplished in a normal and easy way. Sometimes whole fleets of sailboats are seen going around a buoy in this manner. It is when the wind is strong that care must be exercised.

--- HELPFUL HINT ---

A cockpit cover is essential for keeping rain and weather out of the boat when it lies unattended at anchor. It helps keep the inside of the boat dry. Water or dampness in the bilge soaks into the wood, making the boat heavy. A heavy boat sails more slowly and is not as lively a sailing craft as it should be.

Here is an ideal type of cockpit cover for the small sailboat. It is closed in front and open at the after end to allow for ventilation. It hangs over the boom and is fastened in front by a collar around the mast. Lines hold the lower forward ends to the shrouds. The after end is held by a line tied to the boom. Snaps just under the rail hold the sides in place and prevent them from blowing out.

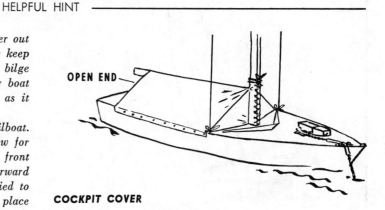

OPEN END

COCKPIT COVER

Controlling the ANGLE OF HEEL
of a small sailboat
for safety, balance and faster sailing

CHAPTER 17

THE angle of heel of a small sailboat is controlled by the crew. They move thwartship—inboard and outboard—to counterbalance any heeling effect caused by the wind (or lack of wind) that interferes with the speed, efficient sailing and safety of a boat. Except under extremely strong wind conditions when wind has to be spilled from the sails for safety, the methods herewith described are most effective in keeping a craft sailing at its proper angle of heel for maximum speed.

Any craft, whether keel or centerboard, should not be allowed to heel more than approximately 30 degrees, because the hull shape, at this angle of heel, offers a resistance to the water which causes the craft to slow down through the action of retarding wave formations.

If the crew, by "hiking out" or leaning outboard from the rail, cannot correct or reduce this 30-degree angle of heel, it is imperative to reduce sail or spill wind from the mainsail. A fisherman's reef (jib sheet taut but main eased) will reduce the effective area of the main. When sailing under extreme conditions, a craft will move faster under shortened sail without extreme heel which, besides slowing the boat, imposes severe strain on rigging, sails and crew.

HEELING IN LIGHT AIRS

When the wind is too feeble to heel the vessel, the boat is purposely tipped to leeward. This is done by moving the crew to the leeward side. The sails will then assume a natural curve and cause whatever air there is to flow easily over them, thus imparting drive. This leeward heel is easily controlled and should never be greater than 10° from the vertical. In a fleet of boats sailing in light airs, those which keep the proper curvature in their sails move faster.

HEELING IN MEDIUM WINDS

In gentle and medium winds the angle of heel is easily controlled and does not present much of a problem. The crew keeps to the center of the boat or moves slightly to the windward side to balance the craft so that it sails at its smallest angle of heel consistent with the sails' holding their proper curvature and the wind flowing freely over them. The crew should keep as low as possible to reduce wind resistance, and should not jump around. The move-

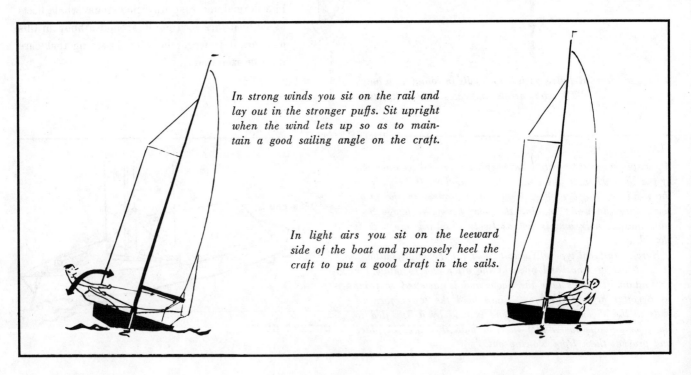

In strong winds you sit on the rail and lay out in the stronger puffs. Sit upright when the wind lets up so as to maintain a good sailing angle on the craft.

In light airs you sit on the leeward side of the boat and purposely heel the craft to put a good draft in the sails.

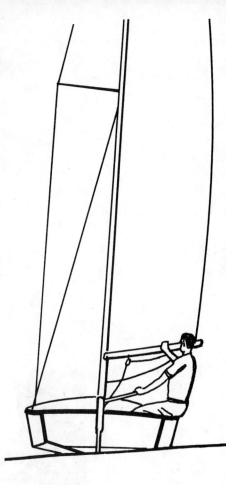

Sailing in very light wind, boat at right is using the proper procedure to create a curve or arc in the sails to get more drive. The man on the lee rail is heeling the boat just enough to incline sails away from the perpendicular and take a form more conducive to better wind flow. About 5- to 10-degree heel is all that is necessary.

ments of all on board should be cat-like; easy and smooth, no jarring or bumping. This also applies whether the wind is light or fresh.

HIKING IN STRONG WINDS

In strong winds, the crew tries to keep the boat upright and sailing fast at as small an angle of heel as possible. The crew sits up on the high or windward side. On a centerboard craft, the more a boat heels the farther outboard the crew leans. Straps running athwartship or along the side of the centerboard trunk (called hiking or toe straps) furnish the toe hold needed to keep the crew from falling overboard. When done properly, this method, called hiking, is most effective for reducing the angle of heel. The counterbalancing body weight can be moved further outboard when gusts of wind exert their extra force on the sails. The crew must be agile and quick to sense any change in wind strength for it is just as necessary to sit upright when a puff lets up as it is to lean out when the gust strikes. This method, of course, is not practical on larger keel boats or on those sailing classes that do not permit hiking straps, such as the Stars. Lying along the weather rail with a firm handgrip then becomes the most effective method of counterbalancing excessive heel.

This, too, is a method used to control angle of heel on larger keel boats when the winds are strong. Crew members lie half over the rail, holding on with one hand, one leg carefully hooked over the side (not dangling), the other stretched along the deck. All of the crew are on the high or windward side of the craft. Because larger, keel sailing craft are steadier, the crew can hold position (except when tacking) and not have to shift weight to counteract every variation in the strength of wind as is necessary with smaller, more sensitive centerboard craft.

The most effective way to maintain an upright position in strong winds is to sit well out on the deck or rail, hooking the feet under a support or strap and leaning out when the unusually strong puffs come along. This quick, easy method, called hiking, allows for the heavier part of the body to extend outboard where weight does the most good, and counteracts the heeling forces created by strong wind pressure on the sails. It also keeps the hands free for quick sheet handling. For best speeds in ordinary winds a boat should not heel more than 10 degrees and should never be allowed to heel more than 30 degrees.

Laying far to windward two expert sailors, with feet securely tucked under straps, show excellent form in keeping their small centerboard sailboat going at maximum speed. Notice how level the boat is riding. The more upright a craft is sailed, except in extreme light airs, the more it will sail on its designed hull lines and thus sail faster. Notice too, how heads of the crew are carefully kept up for continuous observation of the sails, angle of heel and for general awareness of what is going on around them.

HOW MUCH SAIL DOES THE WIND STRIKE
WHEN THE BOAT IS HEELED?

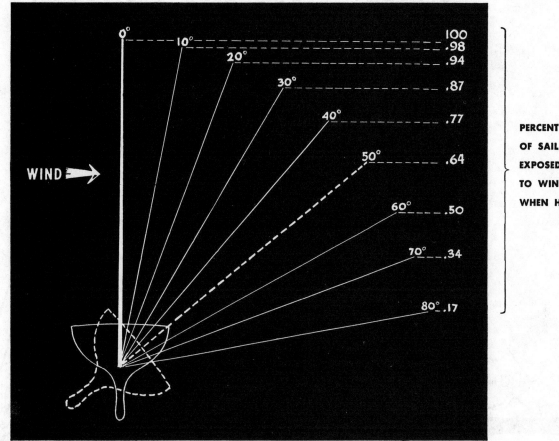

ANGLE OF HEEL

WIND

0°   100
10°   .98
20°   .94
30°   .87
40°   .77
50°   .64
60°   .50
70°   .34
80°   .17

PERCENT OF SAIL EXPOSED TO WIND WHEN HEELED

The angle of heel between 0° and 10° is not vital but the angle between 40° and 50° is very important. The greater the angle of heel, the less sail is exposed to the wind. This is a safety factor because much of this wind spills over the top. However, it cuts down on the effective drive of the sails. Hiking to the high side of the craft when it heels in strong winds not only keeps the boat more upright but keeps more sail in the wind for driving purposes. Great care in handling the boat must be taken when it heels more than 50° although only 64% of the sail is exposed, for it is then a candidate for a knockdown or capsize. Notice that only 2% of sail area is lost when a craft is purposely heeled 10° to leeward.

HELPFUL HINT......USE OF ELASTIC SHOCK CORD

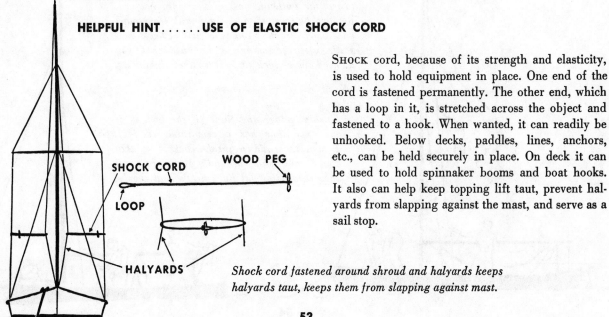

SHOCK CORD

WOOD PEG

LOOP

HALYARDS

Shock cord, because of its strength and elasticity, is used to hold equipment in place. One end of the cord is fastened permanently. The other end, which has a loop in it, is stretched across the object and fastened to a hook. When wanted, it can readily be unhooked. Below decks, paddles, lines, anchors, etc., can be held securely in place. On deck it can be used to hold spinnaker booms and boat hooks. It also can help keep topping lift taut, prevent halyards from slapping against the mast, and serve as a sail stop.

Shock cord fastened around shroud and halyards keeps halyards taut, keeps them from slapping against mast.

Approaching and Picking up the Mooring

CHAPTER 18

1 *On approaching a mooring, if yours is a centerboard boat, drop the centerboard all the way. This gives the boat more stability, aids in steering and gives a steadier forward deck on which the crew can work when mooring.*

Drop the jib, unsnap it from jib halyard, bag it, make jib halyard fast, then coil jib sheets. A note of caution. Some boats, with the mast stepped well aft, may have a tendency to get caught in stays without the jib to assist in swinging the bow. To avoid any trouble, particularly in crowded anchorages, be sure the craft can be readily controlled without the jib. If your boat does not handle with assurance under main alone, keep the jib up until the mooring is secured.

2

4 *Pick up mooring, cleat and make fast the mooring line, making sure the line passes through the chocks. Slip the boom into boom crotch. Haul the mainsheet in tight. Lower the mainsail carefully so that the sail does not go overboard and get wet. Release and unfasten the outhaul, unsnap the main halyard. Remove battens, then the mainsail from mast and boom tracks. Bag the sail. Check halyards after fastening to be sure that you allowed some slack for wet-weather tightening.*

Unship rudder and tiller (if the boat is of the type that has a removable rudder). Fasten these down inside cockpit so that they can't slide around. Make fast all loose gear. Coil all lines neatly and evenly. **5**

IN ALL approaches to picking up a mooring, the idea is to bring the boat to leeward of the mooring float, then to shoot up into the wind to a dead stop alongside of it. Now, merely lean over, pick it up and make it fast to the mooring cleat without undue strain.

In ordinary sailing breezes most skippers learn to do this in an easy and quick manner without fuss or mishap.

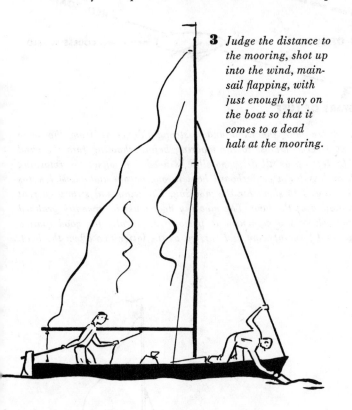

3 *Judge the distance to the mooring, shot up into the wind, mainsail flapping, with just enough way on the boat so that it comes to a dead halt at the mooring.*

The trick is to learn when to start to shoot up into the wind and how far away the boat should be from the mooring float when the luff is started.

The number of boat lengths needed to reach the mooring buoy depends on the strength of wind. Since most small centerboard boats do not have too much forward movement when coming up into the wind, a distance of only one or two boat lengths in light airs, or three in heavy winds, should be allowed (depending on the type of boat).

Keel boats have more forward movement (way) on them when coming into the wind; therefore more distance to the buoy from the luffing point must be allowed. This distance is generally about half again as much as allowed for a centerboard boat.

Whenever possible, at some distance from the mooring, drop the jib, unsnap it from the forestay, and stow in its proper bag.

With the flapping jib out of the way, picking up and cleating the mooring is made much simpler and easier. The jib also stays clean for it is away from the staining drips of the wet mooring and its sometimes muddy pennant. Then too, the helmsman need not be too concerned about which side of the mooring he brings the bow of the boat as the flapping jib will not interfere with the crew member's picking up the mooring float.

Without the jib, the boat does not point as high or go as fast as when it is up. Speed in itself is not important, however, the rate of approach is because allowances must be made for this when shooting to the buoy.

However, in very light airs the jib is often left up, drawing whatever wind it can. Only after the mooring has been cleated is the jib lowered. Then it is carefully gathered in without touching the deck.

In strong winds and tides picking up the mooring is not so easy. The judging of distance and speed is more acute. The maneuvering must be more thoroughly planned if one is to pick up the mooring in a seamanlike manner. It is not uncommon to see skippers miss several times before making the mooring.

Diagrammed on the following pages are the methods to approach a mooring float when running, reaching or beating and also a number of special situations that call for extra good planning.

6

Sponge out the bilge, clean topsides and deck. If any fresh water remains in the vacuum bottle or ice water in the cooler, use it to wipe the varnish work. This takes off the salt water residue and helps keep the woodwork bright. Raise the centerboard all the way up. (On some small round-bottomed boats the centerboard is put part way down. This counters excess swinging and rolling in high winds that may cause them to capsize at the mooring.) Unroll cockpit cover and fasten in place.

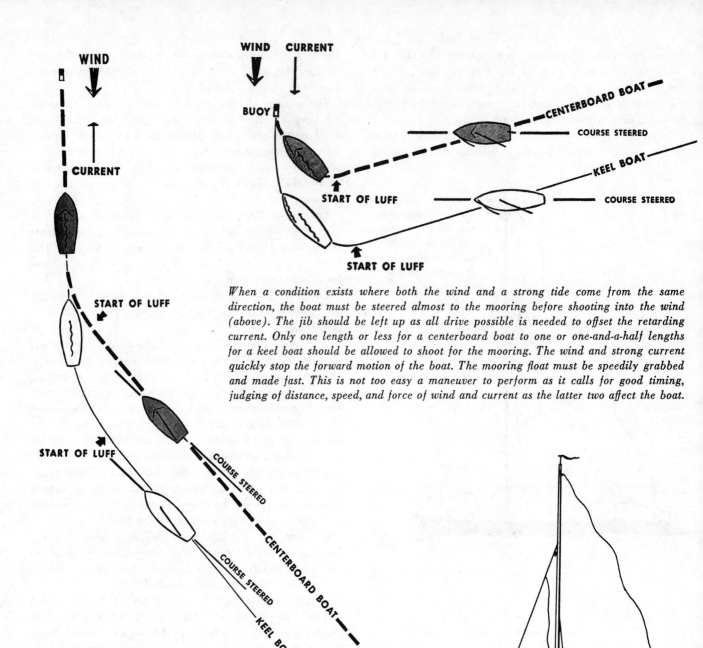

WIND

CURRENT

WIND   CURRENT

BUOY

CENTERBOARD BOAT

COURSE STEERED

KEEL BOAT

COURSE STEERED

START OF LUFF

START OF LUFF

CURRENT

START OF LUFF

START OF LUFF

COURSE STEERED

CENTERBOARD BOAT

COURSE STEERED

KEEL BOAT

When a condition exists where both the wind and a strong tide come from the same direction, the boat must be steered almost to the mooring before shooting into the wind (above). The jib should be left up as all drive possible is needed to offset the retarding current. Only one length or less for a centerboard boat to one or one-and-a-half lengths for a keel boat should be allowed to shoot for the mooring. The wind and strong current quickly stop the forward motion of the boat. The mooring float must be speedily grabbed and made fast. This is not too easy a maneuver to perform as it calls for good timing, judging of distance, speed, and force of wind and current as the latter two affect the boat.

In a situation like the above, where wind and strong tide are opposing each other and the tide has the greater effect on the boat, the basic and safe way to approach the mooring is to drift down it. Luff at a point 4 or 5 to 6 or 7 boat lengths away (depending on type of boat) when shooting for the mooring float. Ordinarily these distances are too great to bring the craft to the float, but the current in this case will carry it onward after drive from the sails is lost. The skipper has his hands full. He must steer right for the float, be ready to let go the main halyard and gather in the sail the moment the crew has successfully grabbed the mooring. As the mooring is made fast the boat will swing and turn with the current, bringing the stern to the wind. Should the mainsail be left up, the wind will fill the sail and swing it out making it difficult to lower. The craft may also start sailing on the mooring causing it to jibe. The diagram shows the courses sailed and the courses steered, which are of necessity different because of the effect of the strong current on the sailboat.

Shooting into the wind for a landing at dock or float involves same sailing procedures as shooting a mooring—plus need to fend off. Crew should be seated, feet shod.

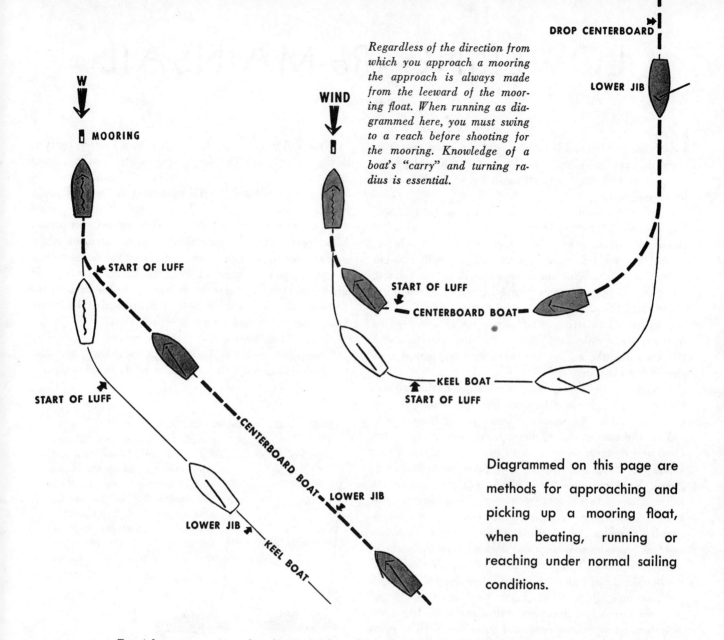

DROP CENTERBOARD

LOWER JIB

W

MOORING

WIND

Regardless of the direction from which you approach a mooring the approach is always made from the leeward of the mooring float. When running as diagrammed here, you must swing to a reach before shooting for the mooring. Knowledge of a boat's "carry" and turning radius is essential.

START OF LUFF

START OF LUFF
CENTERBOARD BOAT

KEEL BOAT
START OF LUFF

START OF LUFF

CENTERBOARD BOAT
LOWER JIB

LOWER JIB
KEEL BOAT

Diagrammed on this page are methods for approaching and picking up a mooring float, when beating, running or reaching under normal sailing conditions.

To pick up a mooring when beating (above left), the craft should first be steered to a point several boat lengths to leeward of the mooring. Then the boat is luffed and steered directly for it (called shooting for the mooring). For a centerboard boat this point is one or two boat lengths away. In all approaches more distance for shooting into the wind must be allowed by a keel boat for it has greater momentum, or carry, through the water. Under normal conditions it is better to have the jib lowered and stowed before the mooring is picked up. The crew then has a steadier, completely clear forward deck on which to work.

WIND

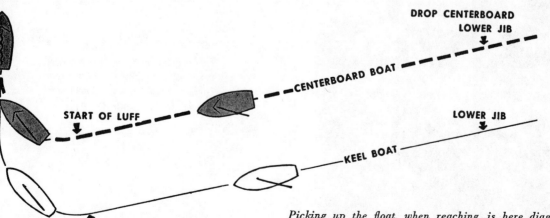

DROP CENTERBOARD
LOWER JIB

START OF LUFF
CENTERBOARD BOAT

LOWER JIB

KEEL BOAT

START OF LUFF

Picking up the float, when reaching, is here diagrammed. Notice that the final shoot for the float is the same in all diagrams on this page. It is the most important part of the well-executed maneuver.

LOWERING the MAINSAIL

CHAPTER 19

BEFORE the mainsail is lowered, put the boom crotch in place and set the boom into the crotch. This keeps the boom from swinging and getting in the way, particularly on a windy day.

Now uncleat the main halyard, but be careful in handling the coil. It must not be thrown aside, any old way, but cleared for running by being placed neatly right side up, so that the halyard leads from the top and will run out without snarling. With one hand controlling the halyard, allow the sail to come down smartly. Use the other hand to guide the folds of the sail over the boom.

Sometimes in a strong wind, due to the violent flapping of the sail, sail slides may stick on the mast track and stop the descent of the sail. A few sharp tugs on the luff rope should free the slides.

After the sail is down, cleat the loose end of the halyard. Never allow the halyard to hang free, for it may run up the mast, and leave you with a sticky job of recovery.

Take the battens out of the sail, lay one on top of the other and tie them together. Stow them carefully in a spot where they cannot be stepped on, broken or kicked overboard. Now unshackle the halyard from the head of the sail and fasten this shackle temporarily to a shroud turnbuckle, a necessary precaution to prevent the halyard from running through the masthead sheave. Release the mainsail tack from the gooseneck and the clew from the outhaul.

Slip the slides off the mast track. When all clear, stuff the head of the sail into the bag and then the rest of it. Pull the bolt rope slides off the boom track and, as the sail is pulled forward off the boom, stuff it in the sail bag. Clew is in last, on top of the heap, and therefore first out when it is next used.

If the sail is wet, don't bag it. Bundle it loosely, carry it to the locker room or take it home where you can hang it to dry.

Release the halyard shackle from the turnbuckle where it had been previously fastened, and fasten it to the gooseneck, or outhaul, depending on which method you prefer. Either place is okay. (Some skippers prefer securing to the outhaul, for should the boom jump out of the boom crotch, as can happen in rough weather, the halyard would hold the boom high and prevent any damage to the deck or the boom.) Take the slack out of the halyard and make it fast. Coil what is left and secure it on the cleat.

Now tighten, cleat and coil the mainsheets.

Unship the rudder, if it is of the portable kind, and stow it. Close up the sail bag, and you're ready to go ashore.

FOR A FREE RUNNING HALYARD

When lowering the mainsail, the halyard should run free. To insure this, the halyard should lead from the top of the coil, as shown in the right illustration and not from underneath the coil as in the drawing on the left. An uncapsized coil encourages halyard snarls. Care should be taken that the coil lies right side up.

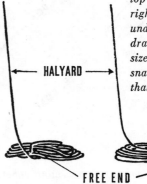

In lowering gaff- or lateen-rigged mainsail, remember that spar comes down with it. Lower sail slowly, in full control.

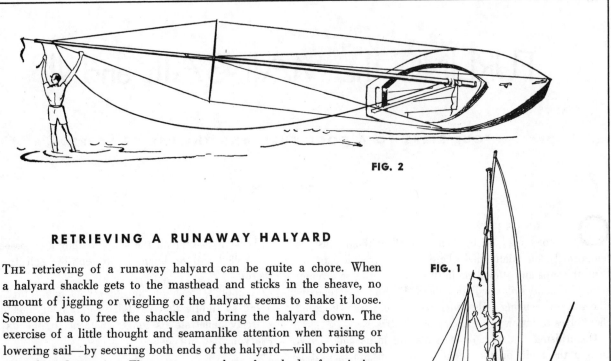

FIG. 2

FIG. 1

RETRIEVING A RUNAWAY HALYARD

THE retrieving of a runaway halyard can be quite a chore. When a halyard shackle gets to the masthead and sticks in the sheave, no amount of jiggling or wiggling of the halyard seems to shake it loose. Someone has to free the shackle and bring the halyard down. The exercise of a little thought and seamanlike attention when raising or lowering sail—by securing both ends of the halyard—will obviate such an awkward situation. There are a number of methods of retrieving. One is to bring the boat alongside a high wharf; another is to heel the boat toward a convenient building roof or a convenient pierside flag pole. (Fig. 1). Third, beach a small centerboard craft and tip it on its side (Fig. 2). (On larger craft where masthead halyards are used for headsails, a bosun's chair can be rigged to hoist a man loft.)

─── HELPFUL HINTS ───

MAKING SAIL SLIDES MOVE EASILY
An occasional rubbing of mast track and boom track with a cloth, on which a fine grade machine oil has been squirted, is of big help in making the sail slides move easily. This can be quite an aid when lowering sail, for it allows slides to slip down easily and quickly without jamming. This can also be an important factor when sail has to be lowered quickly, as in a squall.

Rubbing oil on the jib stay will also help the snap hooks to slip up the stay or slide down without catching.

LOOK ALOFT, CHECK LINES
Before sail is lowered or raised, the skipper should look aloft to see if halyards are clear or whether the sail is fouled on the topping lift. Halyards should lead clear from the sheave aloft down to that part in the sailor's hand and not be involved with other lines or shrouds or stays. The crew should stand clear of any coils that lie on deck and thus avoid getting caught in the bight of a running line.

CLEANING LINES
At the end of the season, take the lines that have been removed from the boat and place them in a large pan of luke warm water into which some mild detergent has been poured. Allow them to soak for at least half a day, or at least long enough for all the salt and dirt to work out from the fibres. Stir the water every now and then to help in the cleansing action. After being thoroughly soaked remove from pan and wash clean in fresh water. Spread the lines out loosely and allow to dry in the sun. This renews the life of the lines and also cleans them up.

FURLING the MAINSAIL and JIB

FOUR STEPS TO A GOOD FURL, AND THE USE OF STOPS

CHAPTER 20

Occasions may arise when a small sailboat must be temporarily left unattended where it is not practical to unbend the sails and stow them in their bags. In these circumstances a good sailor will furl them. Furling is a seamanlike way of securing sails and keeping them from flogging themselves to tatters if a sudden squall strikes.

On cruising craft where the sails are large and heavy, furling the main on the boom is common practice. It is normally protected by sail covers when left for any time.

There are four steps to a good furl: (1) insert the long narrow ties called stops; (2) lower the mainsail and remove the battens; (3) roll or furl the sail; and, secure it with the stops.

Before the sail is lowered, stops are tucked *between the sail and sail track* and allowed to hang as shown in Fig. 1. (Sometimes a loose half hitch is put to hold them in place.) One stop is placed close to the gooseneck and another forward of the outhaul. Others are spaced evenly between. The number of stops used depends on the length of the boom. On a sailboat of 20 feet or less, four or five will be enough for the mainsail.

After all of the stops have been run through, the mainsail is lowered. The folds of the sail are arranged neatly on the boom (Fig. 2) then pulled or stretched aft. This removes any wrinkles or unevenness in the folds. Battens are removed unless the boat is going to be used again that day. Care must be exercised when battens are left in their pockets to see that they lie parallel to the boom; otherwise they may be broken.

Now all of the sail is pulled to one side of the boom and allowed to lie on the bottom-most, and largest, fold which has been pulled out to receive all of the folds. (Fig. 3.) Then the sail is tightly rolled, neatly and evenly, with the bottom fold always on the outside. (Figs. 4 and 5.) To prevent bunching of the folds they are pulled aft as they are rolled. The sail is rolled up until it comes to rest on top of the sail track (Fig. 6). It is to be held there firmly by the stops and not allowed to slip to either side of the boom.

The fourth step is securing the rolled sail. The stops are in place, handy and ready for use (Fig. 7). Their ends are brought up and crossed *over* the rolled sail (Fig. 8) and pulled tight. Now they are passed and crossed *under the boom* and again pulled tight (Fig. 9). Again the ends are brought up to the top of the roll and firmly tied with either a square knot or a slippery reef knot (Fig. 10).

Tension is kept on the stops as they are passed around the rolled sail or boom to prevent the sail from losing its roll.

A good seaman of the old school could furl and stop a sail so tightly that hard-driving rain or moisture could scarcely penetrate its folds. That was in the days before everyone had sail covers.

FURLING THE JIB

The first step in furling a jib is to get a few stops from the ditty bag. Tuck them separately in your belt or through your trouser belt loops so they are handy and easy to pull out when needed.

Release the jib halyard and lower the jib. Still holding the halyard, transfer the shackle in the head of the sail to the clew. Now haul on the halyard till the clew is well off the deck. Cleat the halyard.

Roll up the sail, keeping it as tight and even as possible. A sail is stopped not only to keep it from flying around in the wind but to keep it off the deck. A properly furled jib gives a seamanlike appearance to the foredeck.

Holding the rolled sail with one hand, pull a stop from your belt and wrap it tightly around the bulkiest part of the sail; twice around before the stop is tied. Then stop the thinner part of the furl. With a third "stop," tie the snap hooks together on the jibstay.

Take the slack out of the jib sheets to keep the sail from swinging. On many yachts, before the sheets are taken up, the clew of the jib is taken to one side, the side opposite to the bow chock through which the mooring line is run. It is then secured by a stop on lanyard to the shrouds. Holding the jib to one side allows for freer work space forward.

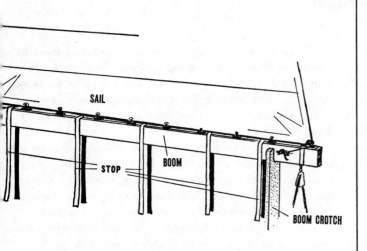

FIG. 1 *Stops are placed in position first before the sail is lowered. They will then be ready to use when it comes time to secure the furl. This avoids last minute scurrying around.*

WHAT IS A STOP?

A STOP is a tie, a long, narrow strip of sail fabric used for holding things in place. Stops for small boats generally measure one inch in width and two to three feet in length. On larger craft they measure as much as two or three inches in width and six feet in length. The edges are doubled over and sewn to prevent tearing and make them more durable.

Substitute stops can also be made from short pieces of line whose ends have been served to keep them from raveling. These are rarely used in permanent furls because they cut into the cloth when tightened and can put ridges in the sail. Wide canvas, dacron or nylon stops lie flat and leave no sharp indentations in the sail.

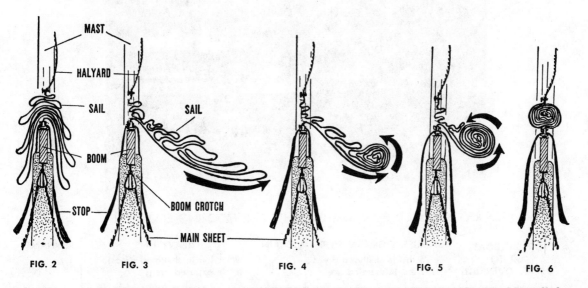

FIG. 2   FIG. 3   FIG. 4   FIG. 5   FIG. 6

The above drawings show in sequence how the sail is first flaked down on the boom (Fig. 2) then pulled out to one side (Fig. 3) and tightly rolled (Figs. 4 and 5) to finish on top of the sail track as a smooth furl (Fig. 6).

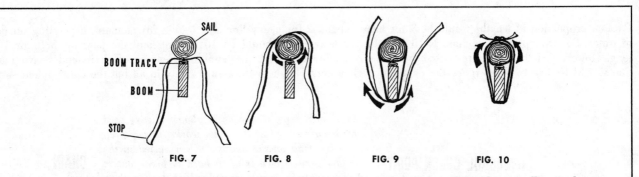

FIG. 7   FIG. 8   FIG. 9   FIG. 10

How a stop is tied around a furled sail. First it is passed between the sail and the sail track, as in Fig. 7 above. The ends are then brought up, crossed over the sail, then down and crossed under the boom, Figs. 8 and 9. Fig. 10 shows how the ends are again brought up over the top and firmly tied into a square or slip knot.

MOORING the Small Sailboat

CHAPTER 21

A MOORING comprises several parts: (1) the mushroom anchor; (2) the cable which consists of heavy chain and line; (3) the mooring pennant, and (4) the mooring buoy or float. All these parts are held together in one continuous line by shackles or splices. The strengths and lengths of all these parts should depend on the size and type of boat to be secured. The larger the craft, the heavier the chain, lines and anchor must be. When there is doubt as to what sizes or weights are to be used, the heavier or larger size should be selected. A good, strong mooring assures the safety of the boat when the skipper is not on board.

In making up a mooring it is best to follow local practice or your yacht club rules.

Marine dealers often make and sell a complete mooring that meets local conditions and approval. Some yacht clubs with crowded anchorages restrict cable lengths to twice the depth of high water, but where there is much swinging room, mooring length should be at least five times the depth of water.

Mooring floats should be painted in distinctive colors or markings and the name of the boat lettered on. This is particularly important when moored at a crowded anchorage, where many of the floats may be of the same shape or color making recognition of your own mooring difficult.

A fluorescent band fastened on a float will reflect the beam of a flashlight at night, helping to furnish quick recognition as to the location and ownership of the mooring.

RECOMMENDED SIZES AND WEIGHTS FOR MOORING EQUIPMENT

	MUSHROOM ANCHOR	CHAIN	HEAVY LINE	PENNANT
FOR SAILBOATS UP TO 25 FT. OVER ALL	75 lbs. in sheltered areas 125 lbs. in exposed areas	5⁄8″ dia.	½″ nylon in sheltered areas; 5⁄8″ in exposed areas	3⁄8″ nylon
FOR SAILBOATS 25 TO 30 FT. IN OVERALL LENGTH	150 lbs. in sheltered areas 200 lbs. in exposed areas	¾″ dia.	5⁄8″ nylon 1″ dia. impregnated with a water repellent	3⁄8″ nylon

PROPER proportion of lengths would be 3 for heavy chain, 2 for heavy line and 1 or 2 for pennant, depending on depth of water. For example: if the chain is 15 ft. long, the heavy line should be 10 ft. long and the pennant 5 ft. or 10 ft. long. However, if there is unrestricted swinging room for the craft, the combined lengths of chain and heavy manila line should be five to seven times the depth of high water. This helps to assure safety in all but the most violent storms.

Mushroom type of anchor is almost always used for mooring because it readily works its way deep into the mud on the bottom. When buried in the mud the mushroom is often hard to break out at the end of the season, so difficult that often it requires special strong lifting apparatus to raise it.

OVERHAUL CHECK POINT

SHACKLE

CHAIN

MUSHROOM ANCHOR

← MOORING FLOAT

OVERHAUL CHECK POINT → **← ROPE SPLICE**

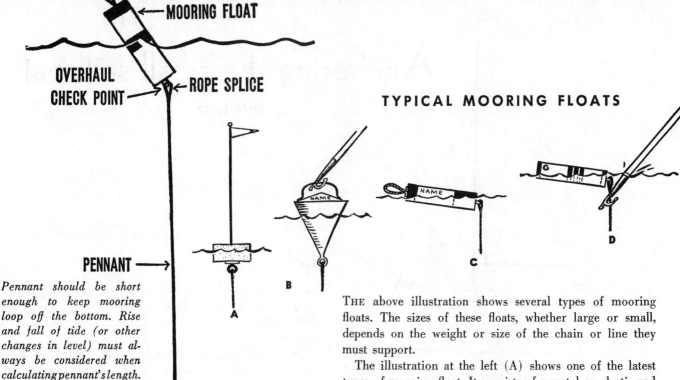

PENNANT →

Pennant should be short enough to keep mooring loop off the bottom. Rise and fall of tide (or other changes in level) must always be considered when calculating pennant's length.

OVERHAUL CHECK POINT → **← ROPE SPLICE**

Below: Parts that connect chain with heavy nylon line. Notice that the eyes or holes in the pins are bound with wire to keep the pins from turning and loosening which they will do if not held tightly. The wire should be of the same metal as the shackle, for example: if the shackle is galvanized the wire also galvanized.

HEAVY LINE →

For safety, boatmen should use new rope (preferably nylon) every year. Manila may lose its tenacity and strength when immersed in water for long periods of time. Also, marine life attacks the fibers causing quick disintegration.

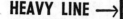

HEAVY MANILA LINE
ROPE SPLICE
METAL THIMBLE
SHACKLE
WIRE WRAP AROUND TO KEEP SCREW FROM TURNING
SWIVEL
SHACKLE
CHAIN

OVERHAUL CHECK POINT **ROPE SPLICE**
SHACKLE
← SWIVEL

THE above illustration shows several types of mooring floats. The sizes of these floats, whether large or small, depends on the weight or size of the chain or line they must support.

The illustration at the left (A) shows one of the latest types of mooring float. It consists of a metal or plastic rod extending about three feet above the water. It passes through a float and, at its lower end, forms a heavy ring to which the mooring pennant is secured. The weight of the mooring pennant helps to keep the rod upright. Sometimes a small flag is attached to the rod for identification.

No boat hook is needed to pick up this float: the crewman, reaching overside, grabs the rod and hauls it up to get at the mooring pennant.

Illustration (B) shows the can-type buoy still much in use. There is a metal strap at the top of the can which the boat hook snags when lifting float from the water. This strap also serves as a carrying handle when the buoy has been brought to the deck.

The can-type buoy comes in different shapes: some round like a ball, others more cylindrical like a large can. Many have a rubber or canvas padding around their widest part to prevent the buoy from scarring the boat's hull.

Illustration (C) shows the float usually used by small sailboats. A rope loop is fastened to the free end for easy picking up. The float usually is made from a piece of lightweight wood (sometimes balsa), 18″ to 20″ long, and painted to stop, as much as possible, saturation by the water. By the end of the season, though, it often becomes water-soaked, barely keeping its top end afloat. It is an inexpensive float, easy to make, and serves its purpose well.

Illustration (D) is similar to (C) but differs in the manner in which it is picked up when a boat hook is used. The hook is pushed under the float and catches the mooring pennant. Both pennant and float are raised together.

Anchoring the small sailboat

CHAPTER 22

Lower anchor over the side of the boat carefully. See that the line runs free and easy. Keep feet away from rope coil. As the boat begins to drop back put the line through the bow chock and let it run out slowly. Do not throw the anchor and line out at the same time, for the line may snarl the anchor and so prevent the anchor from getting its proper grip on the bottom. Besides, you may accidentally get fouled in the line.

Scanning an anchorage, as the crewman in the photograph at left is doing, to locate the best possible place to anchor, is preliminary to many other factors. It is not always advantageous to anchor where other boats already are anchored. Depth of water, the sheltered side of the harbor, wind direction, wave strength, and proximity to facilities ashore must all be considered. Boats anchored first have 'prior rights' and cannot be expected to move if you anchor close to them.

THERE are many factors involved in the anchoring of a boat. All of them are important. Seamanlike procedures and intelligent use of good equipment will make the craft safe and secure.

On approaching an anchorage, the first thing to do is to scan the harbor or area where you wish to anchor. Sail back and forth to find the best spot, the best location, in the quiet side, out of the wind and sheltered from troublesome waves. Generally, there is very little trouble in finding such a suitable site for a small boat. Because of its shoal draft, it can readily anchor in water that is much too shallow for larger craft. Due allowance should be made for the rise and fall of the tide, if any.

However, if the anchorage is crowded, the spot to choose to anchor should be among boats of your own general size, and at least three or four boat lengths away from the nearest boat, whether that boat is ahead, astern or on either beam. This allowance gives you ample free swinging area should the wind change or the tide turn. Should you anchor among larger boats, allowances must be made for their greater swinging radius.

Having chosen your spot, the next thing to do is to come up into the wind and drop the jib. Unsnap the jib from the forestay and stow it in its bag out of the way in the cockpit. This clears the foredeck for the action necessary to the proper handling of the anchor.

Bring out the anchor and anchor line and, if not already fastened together, do so with the knot called the anchor bend. Take the anchor and line, along with a sounding lead, to the foredeck.

It is generally agreed that under most weather and sea conditions, regardless of depth of water, the best holding is when the scope is 7 to 1. Seven lengths of anchor line are let out, one length corresponding to the depth of water at the anchorage as measured from the bow chocks. Shorter scopes of 2 or 3 to 1 cannot, generally, be relied upon to hold when the wind blows strongly.

In the illustration at right, the crewman is allowing the anchor line to run out so that there will be a scope of 7 to 1 (7 times the depth to the bottom as measured from the bow chocks.) In normal pleasant weather the chance of dragging the anchor is negligible. In rough weather, anchoring procedure must be carefully carried out to insure the safety of the craft. The more the wind blows the more anchor line should be let out. Anchor line acts like a spring, taking up the shock when the vessel jumps and pitches in rough water. The longer the line, the more spring it contains, especially nylon.

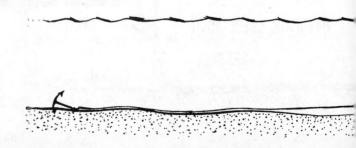

...nchor line neatly coiled and carefully arranged with the anchor in ...manlike manner so that they can be easily lowered into the water.

There are several ways to determine the depth of water. One way is to take a sounding with a sounding lead. Another way is to put fathom markings (6 feet equals 1 fathom) on your anchor line. This way the anchor line is also the sounding line.

When you feel the anchor touch bottom look for the nearest mark on the anchor line, at a height equivalent to the bow chocks. Then knowing the depth, accurately measure out six more equal length of line. You then have enough for the proper scope. In some parts of the country, skippers carry poles, six to eight feet long. These poles usually have foot markings on them, for measuring depth of water.

One of the tricks in anchoring is to drop the anchor in the right spot. When you drift back, allowing the proper scope, you should be exactly the three or four boat lengths you planned to be from the nearest boat.

However, before all this line is allowed to run out, let only two or three lengths run, then snub the line around the anchor cleat. When the craft comes to a halt in its backward drift, the pull on the line will dig the anchor in.

Only then, let the rest of the line out, but pass it out slowly as the boat drifts back. When all the necessary line has been let out, again snub the line around the anchor cleat. Another firm tug will make doubly sure that the anchor has dug in well and is holding. Now make the line fast to the anchor cleat, belaying the end.

Check your position relative to nearby boats, particularly those ahead and astern. If your anchor drags, the space between boats will change. If it remains the same, the anchor is holding.

Of course, should the boat drift because the anchor is not holding to the bottom, you should immediately haul it up and try another spot some distance away where the anchor will hold.

Before fastening the anchor line to cleat, pull or tug on it to test whether the anchor is holding.

FACTORS THAT MUST BE TAKEN INTO ACCOUNT WHEN ANCHORING:

1—Protection of craft from wind and sea

2—Depth of water

3—Rise and fall of tide (if any)

4—Turning circle in relation to other boats should wind or tide change

5—Nature of bottom

6—Scope of anchor line

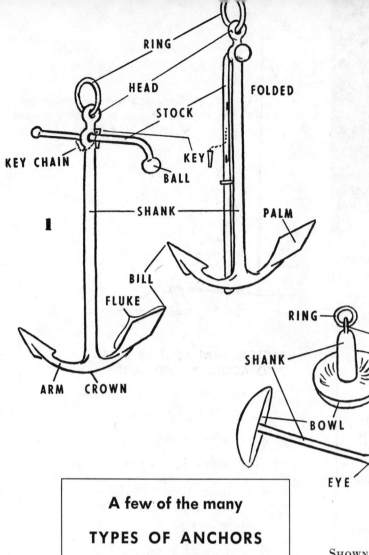

RING

HEAD

FOLDED

STOCK

KEY CHAIN

KEY

BALL

SHANK

1

PALM

BILL

FLUKE

ARM   CROWN

RING

HEAD

SHANK

BOWL

2

EYE

The proper way to lower an anchor. It is being lowered gently into the water. Care is taken that the flukes do not gouge the topsides. The anchor line, on deck, is neatly coiled so that it will run out easily. Notice how the feet are placed so as not to interfere with the line, when it starts to uncoil.

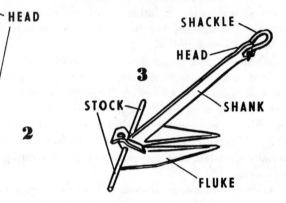

SHACKLE

HEAD

3

STOCK

SHANK

FLUKE

A few of the many
TYPES OF ANCHORS

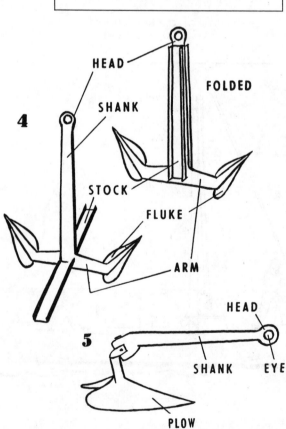

HEAD

FOLDED

SHANK

4

STOCK

FLUKE

ARM

HEAD

5

SHANK   EYE

PLOW

SHOWN here are only five of the many types of anchors available for holding the small boat. All of them are good, in the proper bottom.

It is better to use the type of anchor that is most popular in your area, for through trial and error, that has been found to be the best for holding. They all come in various weights and sizes. The lightest ones, of course, are used for the smaller boats.

Notice that the names of the parts of the anchors are similar even though the anchors are different in appearance.

1. The old reliable YACHTSMAN'S ANCHOR opened for use and, at the right, ready for stowing.

2. Two types of MUSHROOM ANCHORS, similar except that one has a heavy short shank, the other a long thinner shank. Lines are less apt to snag on this type when stowed in the boat, because there are no flukes to catch on to. Mushroom anchors hold well in soft muddy bottoms.

3. The DANFORTH ANCHOR is light in weight in proportion to its exceptional holding power. Because of its small size and good holding qualities when used with proper scope, it has become very popular.

4. The NORTHILL ANCHOR is also small and light in weight for its holding power, therefore easy to raise and lower. Its double stock is folded against the shank when stowed.

5. The PLOW ANCHOR digs sharply and buries itself in the sea bottom. If improperly lowered it will right itself when strain is put on the anchor line.

LEAVING THE ANCHORAGE

THIS is similar to leaving a mooring except that here we have an anchor and anchor line to contend with. These are the steps to be taken in getting underway:

(1) Shorten scope of anchor line so that it is almost vertical. (1 and 2 in illustration below.)

(2) Hoist mainsail but leave boom in boom crotch, unless experimentation has proved that the craft behaves better with the boom free.

(3) Haul up the anchor.

(4) When anchor comes above water, hold it there so it can be cleaned, if muddy, with swab or sponge or by dunking up and down in the water. When clean, raise anchor to deck.

(5) Coil anchor line and stow below decks together with anchor.

(6) Unbag jib and snap it to jib stay. Attach the jib sheets. While all this is going on watch your drift.

(7) Remove boom crotch, let mainsheet run.

(8) Raise jib, then put jib aback and bear off in desired direction.

NOTE: This description is conditioned on there being adequate sea room and is the normal and proper procedure to follow. However, when an anchorage is overly crowded it may be imperative to quickly raise the jib, item 8, after the anchor has been raised for full control of the craft. Completion of items 4 to 7 can then wait until the craft is clear of other boats.

TYING THE ANCHOR BEND

(Also known as the FISHERMAN'S BEND)

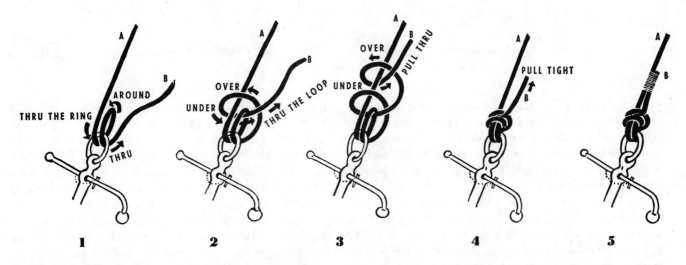

(1) *Take the end (B) of the line, pass it through the ring of the anchor, then around and through the ring again, forming a loop (known as a round turn).*

(2) *Next take the end (B), pass it over the long part (called the standing part) (A), then under and through the loop that was formed in illustration No. 1.*

(3) *Now, again take end (B), pass it over and under (A),* and then through the loop just formed and pull through.

(4) *Take the end (B), and pull so that all parts of the knot are snug and tight.*

(5) *If anchor line is to be left tied permanently to the anchor, a good sailor will tie the loose end (B) to the standing part (A), so as not to leave it dangling. Binding of one line to another with a light twine is called seizing.*

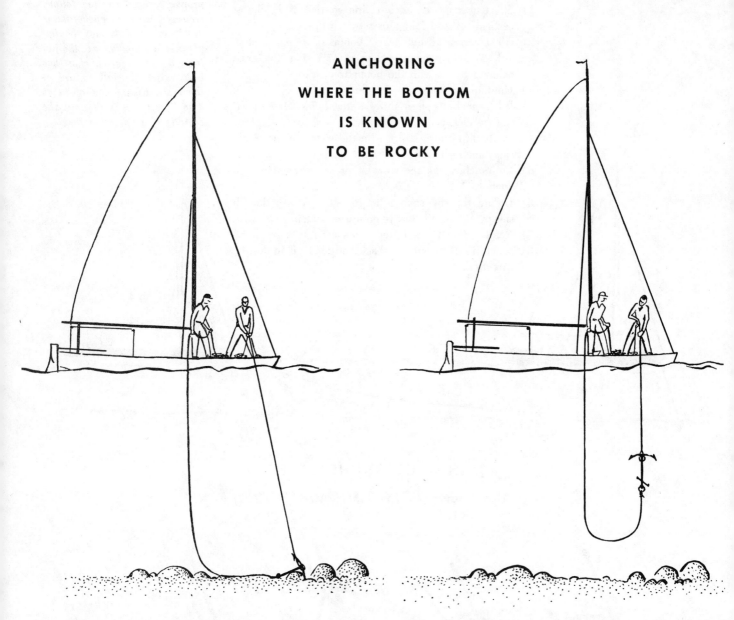

ANCHORING WHERE THE BOTTOM IS KNOWN TO BE ROCKY

SHOULD the anchor be dropped where a bottom is known to be rocky, the anchor flukes may catch under a rock and be held fast. It is a wise precaution when anchoring in such a spot to tie a line to the crown of the anchor. With this line you will be able to lift and draw the anchor out crown first should it be stuck.

This line can be rigged in a number of ways. 1. From the crown to a float. The line is just long enough to reach the surface of the water (allowing for any rise in tide). 2. From the crown to the anchor cleat on the foredeck of the boat. Here the line should be several feet longer than the anchor line, for it should not take any strain, but be left hand loose. 3. A line, slightly longer than the depth of water, one end of which is fastened to the crown, the other end tied as far up to the anchor line as the length will allow. 4. Sometimes by "scowing," that is, by attaching the end of the line to the crown of the anchor and leading the

line back along the shank to the ring where it is tied with twine. If the anchor is fouled, a strong vertical pull will part the twine, and draw the anchor out crown first. *Scowing should be used only when someone is on board the craft, in constant attendance. It should never be used when the seas are rough, for the tugging on the anchor may break the binding, causing the boat to drift.*

Sometimes it is possible to break an anchor free by "sailing it out." This is done by raising all sail, then sailing in a complete circle, yet constantly maintaining full strain on the anchor by keeping the anchor line taut. The pulling, turning effect created can twist the anchor loose.

If you are a skin-diver, there is nothing simpler than putting on the fins, adjusting the mask, and jumping overboard. Follow the anchor line down to the stuck anchor and free it.

SWINGING CIRCLE OF ANCHORED BOATS

AN anchored boat's swinging circle is the area in which a boat can swing completely around at extreme anchor line length. The small sailboat should always try to anchor in relatively shallow water. By so doing, less anchor line for required scope is needed. This in turn reduces the diameter of the swinging circle and lessens the chance of fouling nearby boats should a wind shift or tide change occur. Below are two diagrams showing the swinging circles of two small sailboats. In illustration A, they are properly anchored. In illustration B, a small sailboat and a larger craft are improperly anchored as to relative distance from one another. The smaller boat has the shorter scope of anchor line and swings around in the smaller circle.

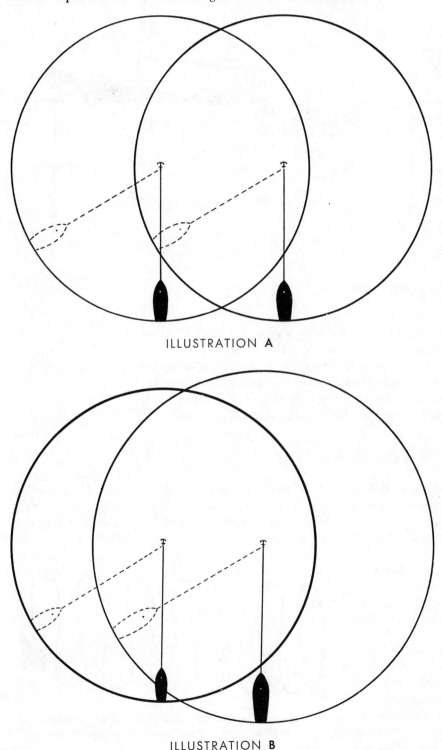

ILLUSTRATION **A**

THE *two black silhouette boat symbols illustrate how two small similar sized sailboats lie when anchored at approximately the closest safe distance from one another. The circles, centers of which are the anchors, represent the respective swinging circles of the two boats. Now, assume the wind shifts 60° or 70°. The boats will swing with the wind. The dotted lines indicate their relative positions after they have swung. They are clear of one another. Both boats can swing all the way around, a full 360°, at anchor line length and still be free from fouling one another. Although the one boat rides over the anchor and line of the other it will not foul them, as the anchor and line at that point are on the bottom. Anchoring another boat length or two away from each other would be still safer.*

ILLUSTRATION **B**

HERE *are shown an average size small sailboat and a much larger vessel lying at anchor (same distance separating them as the two small sailboats in illustration A). They apparently are a safe distance apart. Their respective swinging areas are represented by the two circles. One circle is larger because of the length of boat and the greater scope needed. Again suppose the wind shifts 60° or 70°. The dotted lines indicate their relative positions after they have swung. They are now dangerously close to one another and could possibly foul each other if their movements are influenced by different currents of wind or water. Should the wind shift another 20°, the larger craft, with undoubtedly deeper draft, would override and might foul the anchor line of the smaller one because at that point the line is raised off the bottom.*

Moral: When anchoring among larger craft, allow for their greater swinging circle.

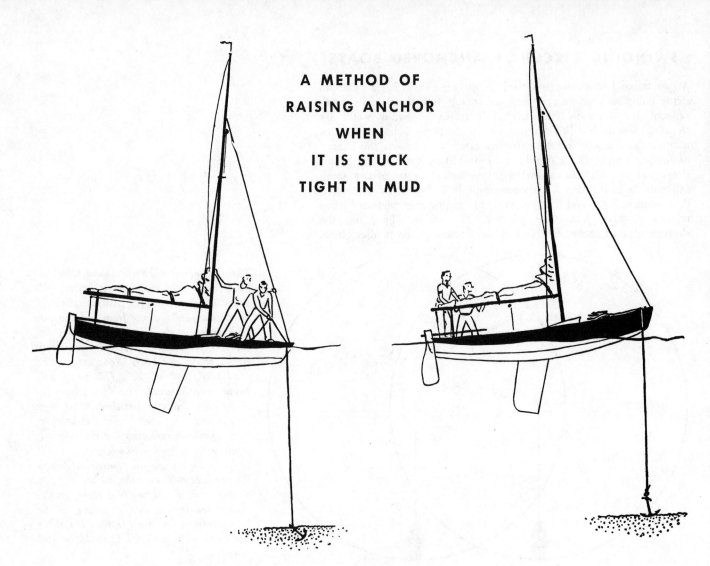

A METHOD OF RAISING ANCHOR WHEN IT IS STUCK TIGHT IN MUD

Should the anchor stick tightly to the bottom so that it can't be raised by hand, here is one method of breaking it free.

Have skipper and crew move to the bow of the boat. Haul in on anchor line until it is taut and as straight up and down as possible, then make fast to the cleat. Now move to the stern. The body weights at the stern lifting the bow, plus the buoyancy of the boat, can break the anchor free.

SOUNDING LINE

A strong fish line, the small ordinary hand line, tied to a 3-pound sinker makes a good sounding line for a small boat. It is compact and easily stowed.

Mark the line in the following manner. Measure off 6 feet (1 fathom) from the sinker end and tie in a marker. The old-timers tied in a single piece of strip leather. There are also numbered tabs available that can be tied to the line instead of leather markers.

Measure off another 6 feet and tie in another marker. Here two pieces of leather are used. This is the 12-foot or 2-fathom marker. Measure another 6 feet and tie in 3 pieces of leather. This is the 18-foot, or 3-fathom marker. These should be sufficient markings for a small boat sounding line where the line is used in anchoring only.

This suggestion is a modification of the sounding line used on larger boats where the lead weighs 5 or 10 pounds and the line is correspondingly stronger. The bottom end

of the lead is hollowed to hold some wax. (This is called arming the lead.) When the line is lowered and the weight touches the bottom, portions of the bottom will adhere to the wax, thus indicating its nature, whether sand, mud, etc.

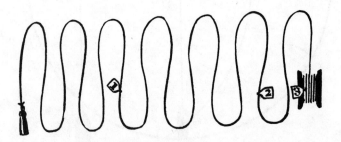

A light strong fish line, with simple obvious markings is perfectly adequate as a sounding line.

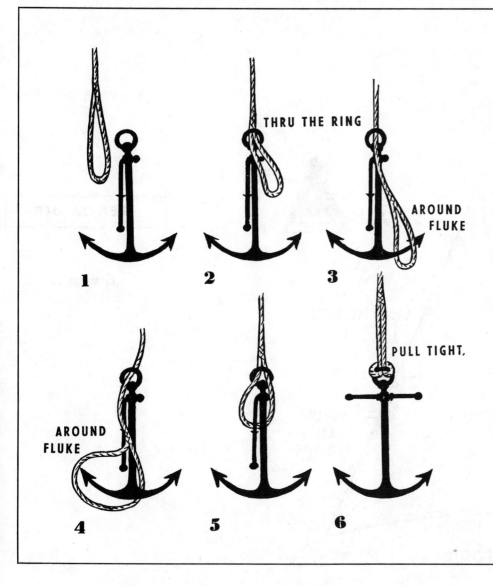

1

THRU THE RING

2

AROUND FLUKE

3

AROUND FLUKE

4

5

PULL TIGHT,

6

Illustrated here is a quick and easy method of fastening a line to an anchor. This can be used with any type of anchor. Follow the illustrations at the left. No. 1 shows the anchor and a line that has a loop spliced in the end of it. In No. 2 the loop end has been passed through the ring, then pulled through far enough so that the loop can be passed around a fluke, as in No. 3. The loop is then drawn over the other fluke, and the line pulled upward as in No. 4 and No. 5. The last illustration No. 6, shows the line pulled tight around the ring.

HELPFUL HINTS

FASTENING SHEETS WHEN SAILING

Do not tie or knot sheets and halyards to cleats when sailing. When rope gets wet, as it often does, it shrinks in length and swells in diameter. This means that knots get so tight and stiff they cannot be united quickly or easily. In an emergency, lines may have to be cut. Lines will hold when properly wrapped around a cleat and can be unwrapped at any time, whether wet or dry, without trouble.

1. Bring the sheet under and around the cleat.

2. Continue on around and cross over the cleat.

3. Now under and around the cleat, then cross over.

4. Then under and around to cross over again; the end can hang loose for the sheet will hold and not slip.

The cleat should be fastened to the deck at a slight angle to the line of pull. This prevents jamming of sheets and allows for easier, faster handling.

71

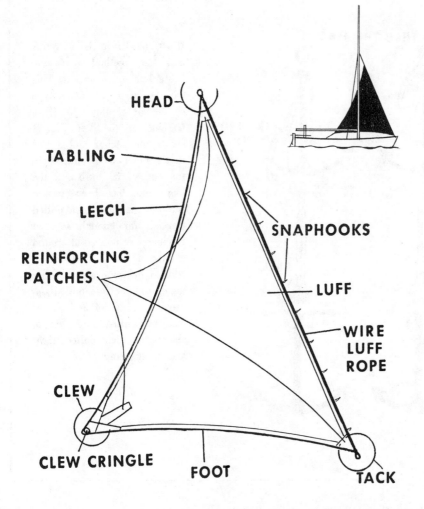

HEAD

TABLING

LEECH

REINFORCING
PATCHES

SNAPHOOKS

LUFF

WIRE
LUFF
ROPE

CLEW

CLEW CRINGLE

FOOT

TACK

Boats of the International Six-Meter Class, pictured here, always carry genoa jibs. These boats are rigged for maximum speed. Their sails are always beautifully cut and shaped, reflecting the best in sailmaking skills and care.

Different craft have different size sails, cut to measurements that conform to class standards. The pictured boat shows a beautifully cut genoa. Notice that the sail cloths are cut differently from those in the mainsail. This is known as diagonal cut and the line running through it from clew to luff is called the miter.

THE genoa jib is also triangular in shape but much larger than the working jib, and overlaps the mainsail. Because of this long foot and the curvature of the canvas, it has to be set outside of the shrouds and sheeted way aft. It furnishes more drive than the working jib and is used for beating and close reaching in all winds but the strongest. Then, either a smaller genoa is set or the skipper goes to his working jib. It is used only on those yachts specifically designed for its use. It sometimes throws a boat out of balance, causing a lee helm, when it is necessary to work the tiller to leeward constantly to offset the yacht's tendency to fall off the wind.

Many modern sloops carry huge genoas. They use them nearly all the time, too, because of the tremendous drive derived from them. But these boats are designed to contend with the extra strong forces exerted and created by this sail. They also have enough crew and equipment to handle it. It takes a lot of beef to handle the sheets in a strong wind, even thought their pull is controlled by a winch. When coming about, the clew of this sail must work itself forward, past the shrouds, and drag itself around the mast. The sheet must be released in ample time for this to

happen. Therefore the boat is brought about much more slowly than with a working jib. Care and judgment, when coming about, must be exercised to prevent the boat from going into irons. The longer, heavier, stronger sheets needed to control this sail act as a drag as they rub against the rigging and prevent the sail from swinging over easily. Often a crew member has to take the clew, run forward with it and lead it around the shrouds and mast to the other side. Sometimes the sheet or the sail itself will snag on a projection, such as a cleat or winch on the mast, as it flaps its way from one side of the boat to the other.

Practically all cruising craft have this sail in their locker and set it when the wind direction and strength are right. Those craft that go in for cruising racing often have a lightweight genoa and a heavy genoa made for use in these respective light and heavy winds. The lightweight genoa generally is a larger sail than the heavyweight. The newer ocean racing yachts are so rigged (the jibstay is run to the masthead) that the sail can extend to the masthead and, when the wind is high, it furnishes tremendous drive. The modern genoa jib resembles a sail used by Italian fishermen operating near the city of Genoa, Italy. Hence its name.

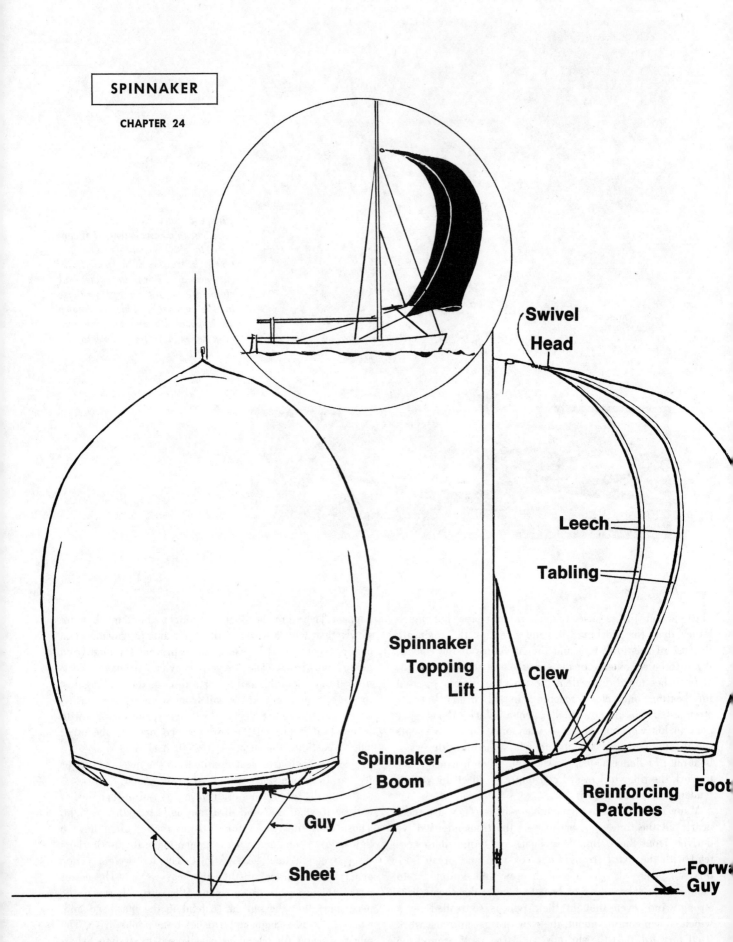

Swivel
Head

Leech

Tabling

Spinnaker
Topping
Lift

Clew

Spinnaker
Boom

Reinforcing
Patches

Foot

Guy

Sheet

Forwa
Guy

A perfect setting, high lifting, spinnaker. Notice the large "shoulders" at the top which contribute much to the efficiency, lift and power of this sail. Both clews are on a line parallel to the deck. This is the way the spinnaker should always be set for best driving power. Raising and lowering of the spinnaker pole keeps this setting constant. The pole is always adjusted up or down to meet the height of the flying clew.

In recent years there has been more experimenting with spinnakers than with any other type of sail. Skippers sensing the extraordinary adaptability of this sail have greatly increased their knowledge of its handling techniques and driving power. Many have suggested methods of jibing that now make this sail easier to handle while racing.

In general, today's spinnaker is an egg- or bell-shaped nylon cloud that billows out at the top and curves in at the sides so as to receive a lift as well as a drive from the wind. Some are more bulbous than others, some spherical, some long and relatively narrow, depending on the fore triangle, the ideas of the skippers and their sailmakers.

The sail is used effectively not only when sailing before the wind but when broad reaching with the wind coming from just abaft abeam. It is effective in very light airs where it does more to keep a boat moving than the mainsail. In strong winds it "pulls like a horse" and care must be exercised in its handling.

Most spinnakers of today are made from the lightest of materials so that they can readily lift and fill out to maximum dimension in the most feathery airs. In this era, the sail is made from very light, very strong nylon.

The parts of the sail as shown in the accompanying diagram are called: the head, at the top corner; and the foot,

The spinnaker shown here is quite different in shape from the others on these pages. It is almost round, and the striping is horizontal. The cloths are cut to put a large belly in the sail without the use of a center, vertical seam. It holds a tremendous amount of wind. The material is as light in weight as fine silk.

Beam reaching under spinnaker, as above, can be tremendously exciting— but often a genoa jib is more efficient on this heading.

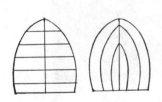 *The diagrams on both sides of this caption show how sail cloths are generally cut to form spinnakers. There undoubtedly are variations of these cuts, one of which appears in a photograph above. Often, alternating colored cloths are used—principally for distinctive decorative purposes, often for ready identification. Some skippers have the upper part of this sail made of dark red cloths and the lower part with the regular natural colored cloths. The theory is that the dark red absorbs heat from the sun and it, in turn, warms and heats the air under it. This, in turn, imparts lift and helps keep the spinnaker high and flying in light airs.*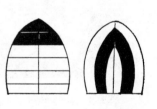

at the bottom edge. Both side edges are called leeches, and both lower corners are called clews. There is no tack, nor is there a luff, except when the sail is set. Around the three sides, as on all sails, is sewn an extra piece of material called the tabling. There are also strong reinforcing patches sewn into each corner. These strengthen the sail and keep it from tearing when under strain.

One corner or clew of this sail, when in use, is held out by a pole, called a spinnaker boom. The other end of this boom is always attached to the mast. To trim for changes in wind direction, this boom can be moved forward and aft or up and down. Its forward or aft movement is controlled by lines called guys. The other corner or clew of the sail is held out, and up, by the wind, but is controlled

by an attached line called a spinnaker sheet.

The after guy and the sheet are interchangeable, depending on which side of the boat the spinnaker pole is set. They usually are the same type of line but are given different names when in use so as to distinguish them in handling. The guy always leads from the clew attached to the spinnaker boom and the sheet always from the other loose hanging clew. The up and down movement of the spinnaker pole which keeps the boom end and clew on a level is controlled by a forward guy, a line led from the outer end of the pole to the foredeck; or a pole downhaul rigged to the middle of the spar, and a spinnaker topping lift, which raises or lowers the spinnaker boom. Both lines, in conjunction with the guy, keep the boom steady.

STORM SAILS

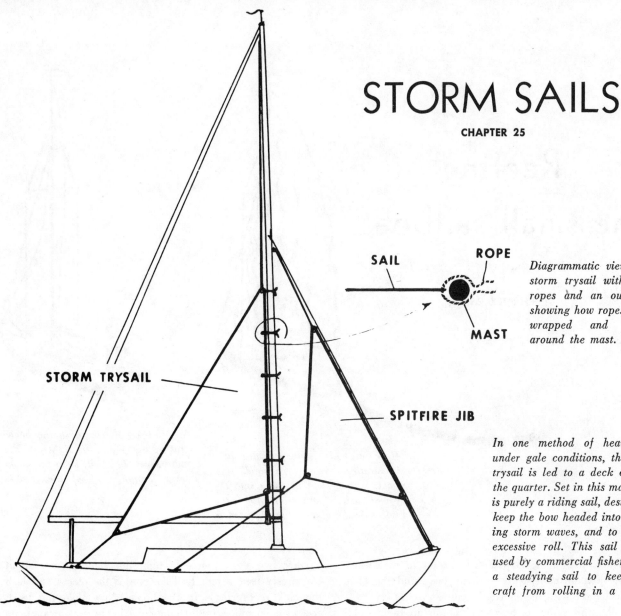

CHAPTER 25

SAIL

ROPE

MAST

SPITFIRE JIB

STORM TRYSAIL

Diagrammatic view of storm trysail with tie ropes and an outline showing how ropes are wrapped and tied around the mast.

In one method of heaving to under gale conditions, the storm trysail is led to a deck cleat on the quarter. Set in this manner, it is purely a riding sail, designed to keep the bow headed into oncoming storm waves, and to prevent excessive roll. This sail is also used by commercial fishermen as a steadying sail to keep their craft from rolling in a seaway.

THE SPITFIRE OR STORM JIB

The storm jib is a cut-down, small-sized working jib made from heavy material to withstand storm winds. Its purpose is to aid in balancing sail area, thereby allowing the boat to steer more easily when sailing under reduced canvas. Small racing craft do not carry this sail because they can easily reach shelter before a storm develops. Almost all cruising boats do carry it because they sail further from sheltered waters and have to sail through whatever weather happens to come along. It is made exactly like a jib and its parts are named after the parts of a jib. Since sail efficiency and drive are not necessary, it sometimes has a bolt rope sewn in the leech to help prevent tearing of canvas. It has a wire luff. Both the foot and the leech are bound with rope which acts as a stiffener and strengthener. When in use it is hoisted high off the deck to prevent any waves from washing into it. It is used usually with a reefed mainsail or storm trysail.

THE STORM TRYSAIL

The storm trysail is a triangular loose-footed sail made from the same heavy fabric as a storm jib. It is a larger sail than the storm jib and is also bound with rope for strength on all three sides. When sail tracks are not strong enough to hold the sail in a storm, lines are sewn at intervals into the luff. When tied they form loops around the mast. When this sail is set as shown above, the boom is lashed down in its crotch. When a large trysail is set in lieu of a deeply reefed main, with the idea of keeping the boat moving on her course instead of heaving to, the sail usually is fitted to go up on the mast track. The clew line is hauled taut aft and made fast to the main boom. The storm trysail's trim is then controlled by the mainsheet.

Reefing
the small sailboat

(Reefing—reducing sail area)

CHAPTER 26

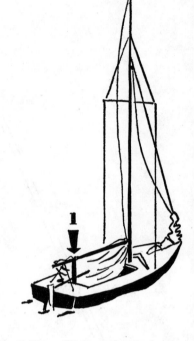

Here are five sequence drawings illustrating reefing of a small sailboat. Above, steer the boat into the eye of the wind and quickly lower the sails. Hold halyards until fastened.

No. 1. Drop the boom in the boom crotch, then haul in tight on the main sheet. This will keep the boom from jumping out of the crotch.

THERE are small-boat skippers who prefer to reef when the winds remain consistently strong. They find the boat easier to handle with the shortened canvas.

Not all small sailboats have reef points in their sails. Many boats are constantly being used for racing, their skippers believing that reef points offer wind resistance and interfere with the smooth flow of air along the sail. They, therefore, order sails without reef points.

Many small-boat racing skippers believe that reefing, as a rule, is not necessary, particularly if the boat can be handled by any of the methods which are described in Chapter 29.

However, larger sailboats, whether used for racing or cruising, do have reef points. It is common practice with large boat skippers to reef when necessary.

Reefing must be done right or the sail will tear and/or pull out of shape.

Here is a good method of doing it. Steer the boat into the eye of the wind, drop the jib and tie or stop it. Put the boom crotch in place and drop the boom into it as the mainsail is lowered. Lower the mainsail all the way, gathering it in as it comes down so that it doesn't fly into the water. Haul the main sheet in tight and make it fast; this keeps the boom from jumping out of the boom crotch. Never leave the mainsail partly hoisted, for it will pull and flap in the strong wind, greatly hindering the operation; besides, the strong wind may fill the sail and capsize your boat.

Have two short pieces of light line handy, each about five or six feet in length. Take one of the pieces and lash the tack reef cringle to the boom. Now take the leech reef cringle, pull straight along the boom and away from the mast. Keep the canvas straight and even with the reef

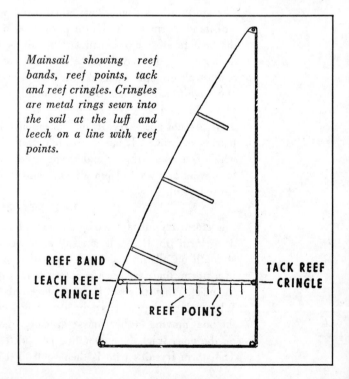

Mainsail showing reef bands, reef points, tack and reef cringles. Cringles are metal rings sewn into the sail at the luff and leech on a line with reef points.

REEF BAND
LEACH REEF CRINGLE
TACK REEF CRINGLE
REEF POINTS

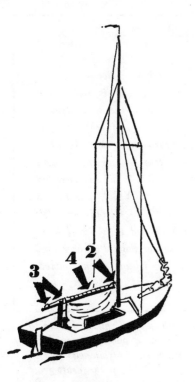

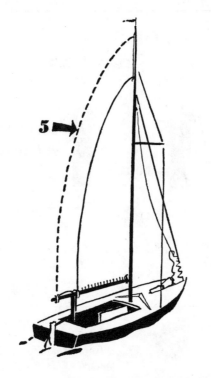

No. 2. Lash the tack reef cringle to boom. No. 3. Holding the leech reef cringle, pull the sail out along the boom. When the sail is stretched taut, lash the reef cringle around the boom. Continue pulling aft, then lash end of line around outhaul and boom. No. 4. Keep reef bands in a line.

Here is shown the difference in sail area: before reefing (dotted line No. 5) after reefing, solid line; a noticeable reduction in area.

Unfasten the mainsheet, raise the mainsail and stow boom crotch, raise jib and then bear off, and you are underway. Keep sheets unsnarled.

bands in a line. With the other piece of line, lash this leech cringle down around the boom, then aft to the outhaul or end of the boom and fasten securely.

Now take that part of the sail between the reef bands and the bolt rope and pull through to the side opposite to that on which most of the sail hangs. Pull this out as evenly as possible and roll up. Form into a nice, neat roll, then tuck between the reef bands and the bolt rope, leaving the reef points free. Tie this roll together with the reef points, using a square or reef knot, but be sure to bring the reef points under the bolt rope (not the boom). Check all of the knots to see that they are tight and in an even line. Now you are ready to raise sail. Unfasten the main sheet; haul on the main halyard and as soon as the boom clears the crotch stow it so that it will not foul the main sheet when the sail fills. Check all the lashings and knots for uneven strain and be sure that all are securely tied. Then take the stops off the jib, hoist and get underway.

If there are more than two in the crew the jib is often left up, the mainsail alone being dropped while the craft is luffing. When the reef is being tied in, the craft is again put on course with the jib full and drawing. Keeping momentum on the craft increases stability and steadies it in a rough and rolling sea.

There is a disadvantage in keeping the jib up with only two in a crew, however, for one has to steer and control the boat. The other has to do all of the reefing and moving about, often having to work with only one hand, as the other is needed to hold on.

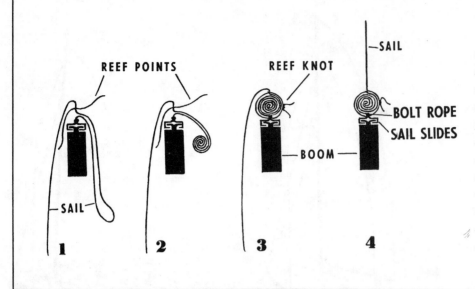

REEF POINTS · REEF KNOT · SAIL · BOLT ROPE · SAIL SLIDES · BOOM · SAIL

1 **2** **3** **4**

Cross section of boom and sail showing how sail is rolled and tied. In No. 1, the sail, between the bolt rope and reef band, is pulled through to the side opposite to that on which the sail hangs. In No. 2, the sail is rolled up neatly. In No. 3, it is tucked between the reef bands and bolt rope, then tied with a reef knot. No. 4 shows the rolled or reefed sail after it has been hoisted.

An all-to-common fault—a slack jib luff. Its cause—failure to raise the jib as high as it can go, or a poorly fastened jib halyard that allowed it to slip when wind strain was put on the sail. This sloppy, scallop effect will keep the craft from pointing as high as it should. The setting of the sails should be checked immediately after a boat is gotten underway, and at intervals thereafter.

─────── HELPFUL HINT ───────

OILING OF SLIDES, SNAP HOOKS, WINCHES AND BLOCKS

The sheaves of all blocks will run better if you oil them every so often, but be careful not to squirt on too much oil so that it drips on the deck or gets over the sheets, halyards, and sails. Just a gentle drop will do.

The slides on the boom and on the mast will slide easier when very lightly rubbed with vaseline. This keeps them from jamming, a serious matter when lowering in a squall.

Right, number 1 shows boom setting in boom notch. Numbers 2 and 3 show where the sail is tied to the boom. No. 4 shows how the reef points are passed under the bolt rope (between the bolt rope and sail track) and then tied in an even, straight line.

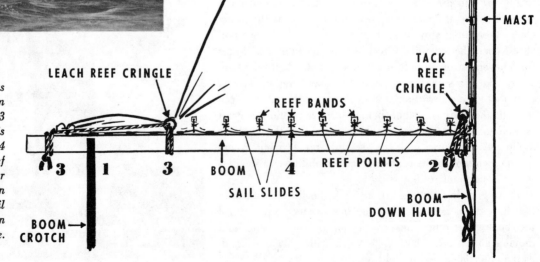

LEACH REEF CRINGLE · MAST · TACK REEF CRINGLE · REEF BANDS · REEF POINTS · BOOM · SAIL SLIDES · BOOM DOWN HAUL · BOOM CROTCH

3 **1** **3** **4** **2**

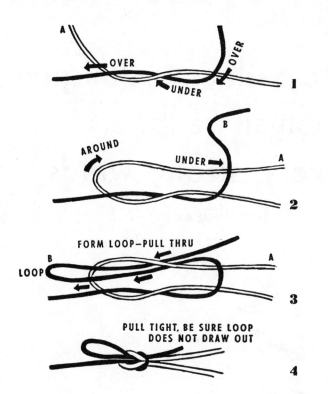

HOW TO TIE THE
SLIPPERY REEF KNOT

As shown at the left (number 1), take the black strand, pass over the white strand, then under and again over the white strand.

Number 2, take end A of the white strand and pass this end under the black strand.

Number 3, form a tight loop with the black strand at point marked B. Pass loop under, then over the white strand, and pull through to hold it in place.

Number 4, hold both ends of the white strand together in one hand, and the black strand loop with the other hand. Pull very tight but be sure the end does not pull all the way through and out.

The slippery reef knot, when tied properly, has an advantage over the regular reef knot, in that it can be quickly untied by simply pulling the loose end. In making, it must be pulled very tight or it will loosen and then open. Should the knot open, unequal and extra strain on the other knots generally results in a torn sail.

HOW TO TIE THE
REEF OR SQUARE KNOT

The reef knot is started in exactly the same way as the slippery reef knot, by taking the black strand, passing it over the white strand and then under and again over the white strand, as at right, number 1.

Number 2, take the end A of the white strand, turn it and pass it under the black strand.

Number 3, take the end of the black strand B, pass it under and then over the white strand, as in this illustration.

Number 4, now hold both ends of the black strand in one hand, and both ends of the white strand in the other hand, pull tight. When tied properly this knot will not open and may even be difficult to untie when wet. It is designed to hold and hold well.

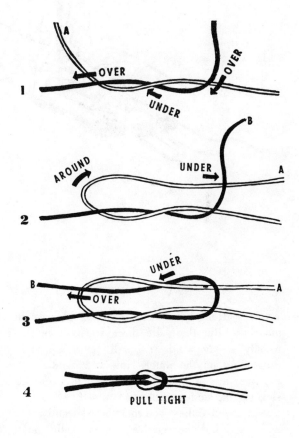

SHAKING OUT THE REEF

Suppose the wind has let up or you're back at your mooring and want to undo the reef. A reef should never be left in any longer than necessary for it can distort the shape of the sail.

Undoing or taking out a reef is called "shaking out." To shake out a reef, go about it in exact reverse order in which the reef was originally tied.

Lower the mainsail, drop the boom in the boom crotch while so doing. Haul in tight on the main sheet and fasten. Untie the reef points first, double checking to see that they are *all* untied. Then untie the outhaul fastening, leech cringle fastening, followed by the tack cringle fastening. Now raise the mainsail so the wrinkles formed in the sail by the reef come out.

Safe sailing techniques for small sailboats in very strong winds

CHAPTER 27

There are two safety precautions to take immediately when hit by a strong puff of wind.

1—Luff up.

2—Let go the sheets, thus allowing the sails to spill the wind.

I N very strong winds small boats should remain at their moorings. But there are times when a sudden and unusually strong wind or squall comes up and you are caught out on the water. How you handle yourself and the boat are of utmost importance to avoid accident to sail, rigging and possibly to yourself.

At times like these you must be constantly alert to wind and wave and the relative actions of the boat. An eye should be kept on the boats to windward, for they get the wind first. How these boats handle themselves will be a clue as to what to expect and what you will have to do when the wind strikes.

The first precaution to take in any sudden strong wind is to luff up. Steer your boat into the eye of the wind. Ease all sheets. If the boat is of centerboard type, lower the board all the way.

If strong winds increase in velocity, drop the sails (mainsail first). If a real black squall appears, drop the sails immediately and run before it under bare poles if the squall brings violent winds. If your boat is moving too rapidly, slow its progress by trailing the anchor warp, or a bucket over the stern.

If ever in doubt as to the force of wind or whether to carry sail or not, drop the sails for safety; the mainsail first, as this has the greater sail area. As the sails come down gather them in, lean on them and hold them down until they are tied up *securely*. If you let them lie loose the wind will get into them, raise them and slam the boat over.

If close to a lee shore, or a hazard of a kind that could damage the boat, or (the exact reverse) the storm is pushing you out to sea, anchor. Let out as much anchor line as possible so the boat rides easily and does not drag.

If the wind continues in force but it is safe to carry some sail, there are a number of ways of sailing safely, which are described on the following pages.

BROAD REACHING

If you have to sail in strong winds, broad reaching is about the safest point of sailing.

Constant play of the sails against the strength of wind will keep the boat in as upright a position as is possible. Let out sheet and luff up in the puffs, bear off and haul in sheet, when the wind softens or lets up. Always try to keep movement on the boat, for that increases stability and maneuverability. Hold just enough sail to the wind for driving power. Both main and jib will be partly luffing, only the after end of both sails will catch the wind and furnish drive to the boat.

"W" with arrow indicates wind direction.

SAILING WITH A TIGHT JIB
AND A LUFFING MAINSAIL

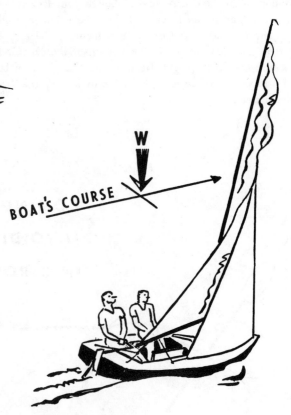

This method is very effective in carrying the boat through the puffs while carrying all sail and still keeping good movement on the boat. It relieves some of the wind pressure on the main, thereby keeping the boat more upright. Let the jib backwind the main. If the jib is allowed to flap furiously it will tear. The main luffs but still has drive in the after end of the sail. Hold the sheets in hands or under a cleat to eliminate the strain on arms.

Be ready to release both jib and main sheets quickly should wind force get too great. Sit up on high side and help balance boat by leaning to windward.

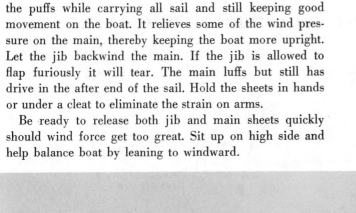

The illustration at the left shows a group of International One Designs racing in a rough sea. The arrows point to the luffing mainsails and tight jibs, one method of sailing through sudden, strong, puffs of wind as explained in the paragraph left above. This method of carrying sail is sometimes referred to as a Fisherman's Reef.

SAILING WITH JIB ALONE

There are several ways of sailing in winds not having the force to require you to drop the sails but still with strength enough to create concern for the safety of boat and crew.

The easiest and safest is probably dropping the mainsail, tying it up and sailing with jib alone. You are then sailing under as short canvas as possible, that is, provided you do not have a storm jib.

It is surprising how well you can reach and often how high you can point with the jib alone. To a degree you have control of the course to sail, though your leeway will be greater than usual. Running before the wind or reaching is much steadier and easier than trying to beat.

Sit on the high side or in the bottom of the cockpit to help keep the boat upright. Do not cleat the jib sheet but hold it in your hands, easing the strain by leading the sheet under a cleat.

COMING ABOUT TO CHANGE COURSE (AVOIDING A JIBE), WHEN RUNNING IN STRONG WINDS AND ROUGH SEAS

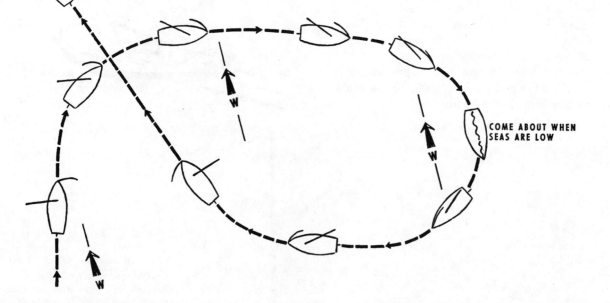

COME ABOUT WHEN SEAS ARE LOW

The action of the sea and the height of the waves play an important part in this maneuver. Generally there are three or four steep, high waves, then a series of short rollers, then three or four more steep ones, and so on. The trick is to luff and come about when the seas run low. Good helmsmanship, good judgment and good timing also play their parts.

Do not come around fast for there is constant handling of straining sheets. Make a big wide loop broad-reaching, then swing to a close reach. Time yourself so that when the seas run low, you quickly come about. When the sails are on the opposite side, let the sheets out (see that they don't snarl) to the point of reaching. Then let out more sheet so as to again run before the wind.

84

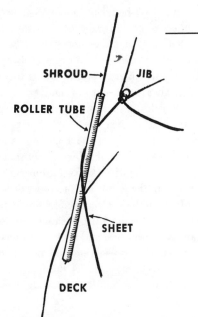

An Atlantic Class sloop sailing through a squall with the mainsail alone. The crew is all on the windward side helping to counteract the extra force in the wind to keep the craft upright. Keeping way on the boat helps control.

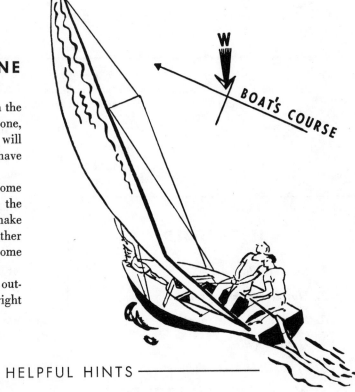

SAILING WITH MAINSAIL ALONE

You have better control of the boat when sailing with the main alone on a reach than when sailing with the jib alone, but more sail area is exposed to the wind. The boat will heel more with the varying force of wind but will have greater speed through the water.

You can luff more easily should strong wind puffs come along. You luff quicker too, for the wind force is on the main alone which in turn has a great tendency to make the bow swing into the wind. This also creates a weather helm, so much so that the boat will automatically come up into the wind should you let go of the tiller.

Keep the crew up on the windward side and lean outward during the puffs to help keep the boat as upright as possible.

--- HELPFUL HINTS ---

ROLLER TUBES ON STAYS.
A plastic roller tube around the shrouds prevents wear and tear to the jib sheets. Because the tube rolls with the pull of the sheet it also makes for easier hauling.

PLACEMENT OF MOORING CLEAT.
Place the mooring cleat close to the mast or splash board rather than at the center of the foredeck. Lines and sails are less apt to snag or get caught by the cleat when placed in this location. It keeps the foredeck clear for action. The crew does not have the worry of tripping over or catching trousers on cleat.

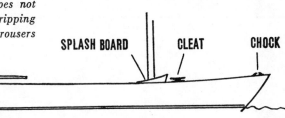

If you should CAPSIZE

Life preservers should be put on whether the crew are good swimmers or not. Besides keeping the crew afloat, life jackets prevent persons in the water from tiring quickly and also keep them relatively warm. Always stick with the boat and try to attract the atention of passing boats.

IF CAPSIZED

1. *Swim to the boat.*

2. *Don life preservers.*

3. *Secure all gear together.*

4. *Get the sail off.*

5. *If possible, right the boat.*

6. *Always STICK WITH THE BOAT. Small centerboard craft will remain afloat though awash.*

7. *Do not swim for shore unless it is close and you are absolutely certain you are a strong enough swimmer to reach it. It is always farther away than it appears to be.*

Generally a boat capsizes when least expected. Sometimes it is unavoidable but more often it is due to a lack of caution, inexperienced boat handling or misjudgment of wind force.

The sudden shifting of wind in a squall or too much wind for the amount of sail carried are the chief causes of upsets of centerboard boats. Other reasons are jibing in a strong wind with centerboard up (or even down) and crew in imbalance (wrong side of boat), or running before a strong wind and sea, where, with crew too far forward, the craft dives into a wave and cannot rise to free itself.

Certain precautions can always be taken to avoid capsizes and those who follow them need never be thrown unwillingly into the water. That doesn't mean one has to be a sissy about the weather, but experienced sailors are always cautious when the weather turns bad or storm clouds form. The inexperienced must always be careful and practice the accepted fundamental rules of safety.

If you do capsize, after getting over the first surprise of finding yourself in the water, swim to the boat and stay with it. The boat will not sink if it is of all-wood construction or equipped with proper flotation tanks or buoyancy material. Make sure that all the crew are accounted for and able to take care of themselves. Occasionally someone may get hit on the head with the boom, get caught under the sail or become entangled with lines, and need assistance. If not already on, get to the life preservers and put them on. Take off sneakers and excess clothing. If the boat gear was not secured properly it will be floating all around you to prevent its drifting away, try to lash the gear together and then fasten the bundle to a cleat or to the mast.

Before attempting to right the boat, the sails must come off. Begin with the mainsail: release the main halyard but make the end fast so it won't get away and entangle swimmers; pull the sail in (down the mast) toward the boat, a slow, difficult job with the sail flat in the water; pull it all the way to the boom, furl it as best you can and secure it with an extra piece of line or the main sheet.

Now do the same with the jib and then make all halyards and sheets fast. You don't want them floating around and getting in the way. Work slowly. Take a breather now and then. Do not tire yourself.

If the centerboard is up, release the pennant so the board can be lowered. The board should be pulled out as far as possible. Now stand on the end of the centerboard and take a grip on the shrouds, a cleat or the rail. Lean backward and push down. One of the crew perhaps can try to push up the mast and tread water at the same time.

The craft should slowly right itself. It will be unwieldy and difficult to control in its swamped condition but it will be able to support the weight of its crew. Climb in over the stern and prepare for the next salvage move.

Don't rush these operations or you will tire quickly. Perform each task slowly and deliberately. Don't forget to look around now and then for passing craft. If one is near, shout as loud as you can and wave a shirt. Skippers of many larger vessels (potential rescue craft) may concentrate so thoroughly on their own compass and steering that they pass within hailing distance without seeing a disabled craft. Try to raise a bright shirt to the masthead where it may attract attention.

Boats with low, uncapped centerboard trunks cannot be bailed out until the slot is plugged (use socks or shirts or sail) because water constantly flows up through the opening. If the sea is rough there isn't much point in bailing be-

Most sailboats cannot be righted until the sails have been brought down, tied to the boom or removed from the spars. The centerboard must also be forced down as far as it will go so the crew can stand on it and furnish leverage for righting the hull. The crew then heaves down and out while holding onto a shroud, a cleat or the coaming. As illustrated below, a crew member can help by going to the opposite side of the boat treading water and giving the shrouds an initial push upward.

FUNDAMENTAL RULES TO PREVENT A CAPSIZE

Precautions to take BEFORE a squall strikes

1. *Head craft into the wind.*

2. *Release all sheets.*

3. *Lower centerboard all the way.*

4. *Lower all sails; furl and stop them.*

5. *Secure the boom in the boom crutch by hauling the mainsheet tight. Haul jib sheets tight and cleat them.*

6. *Secure all gear, including floor boards, that might float away.*

7. *If close to shore or in water that's not too deep, anchor. Do not anchor if you cannot veer sufficient line to insure that the hook will hold.*

8. *Sit on the floorboards.*

9. *Put on life jackets.*

10. *Keep an eye on the weather.*

11. *Locate nearby boats as they may have to help you or you them.*

12. *If running off before a squall in restricted waters, stream the anchor rode and other spare line, or drag a bucket over the stern to slow the boat's progress toward a lee shore.*

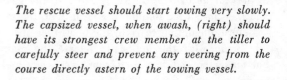

The rescue vessel should start towing very slowly. The capsized vessel, when awash, (right) should have its strongest crew member at the tiller to carefully steer and prevent any veering from the course directly astern of the towing vessel.

cause waves will come aboard. The crew should be lashed to the boat for the beating they take from the waves will soon tire them, precipitate exhaustion and cause grips to loosen.

A boat rarely can be righted—dinghies and board boats excepted—if the sails lie flat in the water. A swamped boat in this position should not be towed. The strains thus imposed can snap the mast and turn the craft upside down. If the mast survives towing but the boat turns bottom side up in shallow water, the spar will stick into the bottom and probably snap.

If a wooden boat has built-in watertight compartments it will ride an inch or two higher in the water than a boat without them. It will also right more easily and be bailed free of water more quickly. Watertight compartments give extra assurance to parents of youthful sailors and an extra safety factor to skippers in trouble.

Sometimes the only thing to do when the weather subsides after a squall is to bail, a slow and tiring project. Do not attempt to climb into the boat until a considerable amount of water has been splashed out and the cockpit coaming is free. When the hull is buoyant enough to hold one person, get him on board carefully. Have him climb aboard over the stern while the others help to balance the boat and keep her from rolling. The one on board should keep in the center of the boat and bail fast. (Hope the bailing bucket was tied on!) The other crew members should get on board as soon as the hull is buoyant enough to hold them. Then all can bail and enjoy the security of being on board.

Keel boats, because of their heavy outside ballast, are more difficult to swamp than centerboarders and only rarely are they capsized. When they are hove down and filled, though, they will sink under the crew unless the craft is fitted with buoyancy tanks or watertight compartments.

Narrow cockpits and wide decks, such as those on Star Class racing sloops, minimize the danger of swamping when the boat takes a hard knockdown; but once the water pours into the hold it is usually a case of "glub-glub."

This boat was awash but had buoyancy enough to hold three teenagers until help arrived. The youngsters followed the rules: put on life preservers; secure all loose floating gear; get the sails down; right the boat and stick with it.

EMERGENCY MEASURES

Should a squall strike suddenly when you are sailing:

RELEASE THE SHEETS

HEAD INTO THE WIND

HAUL THE SAILS DOWN RAPIDLY

LOWER THE CENTERBOARD ALL THE WAY

PUT ON LIFE JACKETS

The bow of a swamped craft, when towed, rises. The water inside the hull sloshes around and rolls from side to side and may cause the craft to yaw. If this yawing is not stopped by the helmsman with corrective tiller action, the craft can again turn over; this time with more destructive results, as the mast may snap.

TIPS FOR RESCUE AND ESCORT CRAFT

Approach and maneuver to leeward of the capsized craft. When its engines are in neutral, the rescue vessel will then not drift down on the distressed boat.

Keep clear of all floating lines; they may snag the propeller.

If the rescue craft has high topsides put a ladder over to make it easier for the wet crew to climb aboard.

Pass a tow line to the crew of the capsized boat, have it led through its bow chock and then made fast to the mast. If the line is made fast to a cleat, the cleat may pull out when strain is taken on the tow line. Get the shipwrecked crew aboard by throwing each swimmer a line and hauling them to the rescue craft one by one.

Pumping a swamped boat seldom helps if the waves constantly wash over her or if the centerboard trunk is not capped or plugged. Many small-boat centerboard trunks are open at the top, allowing water to surge up into the cockpit when the hull is partially submerged.

If they have been in cold water, rub the rescued down with rough towels and cover them with blankets until their shivering stops. Hot drinks help.

If the craft is upright and ready to be towed, put the strongest of her crew back on board to steer. If the centerboard can be raised, the rudder unshipped and all the water pumped out, all of the rescued can stay aboard the rescue vessel because their craft will tow easily without the aid of a helmsman.

Try to pick up all loose floating gear belonging to the capsized craft.

DO NOT TOW FAST—Remember the sailboat is full of water, heavy and sluggish. When towed, strains will be imposed that the boat was not built to stand. Water weighs from 62.4 to 65 lbs. per cubic foot, depending on its salt content. Water in the swamped hull of a small sailboat may weigh close to two tons. The rescue vessel will be towing this extra weight.

TOW VERY, VERY SLOWLY if the craft has not been, or cannot be, righted; otherwise the mast may snap off or be seriously damaged. If at all possible, the stays and shrouds should be released from their deck fastenings so the mast can be removed.

Assign one crew member to watch his craft as she is being towed. The swamped boat may tow erratically and, because of water sloshing around inside the hull, she may turn over again if not carefully handled.

The ACTION of WIND on SAILS

CHAPTER 29

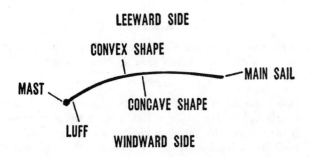

A sail is made to be most flexible. When properly draw-ing in the wind it takes a shape that resembles the upper surface of an airplane wing. The side facing the wind is caused to be concave—the side away from the wind, convex.

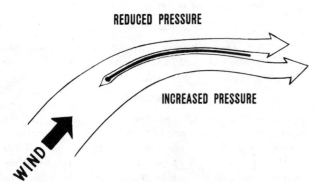

The wind divides as it strikes the sail and is caused to change direction. It develops a positive, increased pressure on windward side—a negative, lesser pressure on leeward.

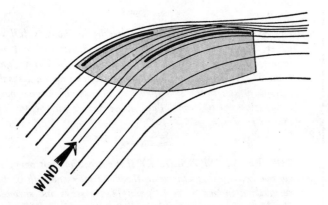

When jib and mainsail are set in proper relation to each other the wind flows evenly and swiftly between them. This creates what is commonly called a "slot effect." The faster the wind flows through this slot, the more the pres-sure on the leeward side of the mainsail is reduced.

THERE is no doubt but that many of the components of a boat help it to move. The hull, the keel, the rudder and sails all contribute. But the one major, controlling factor, the one that contributes the necessary forward drive, is the action of the wind on the sails.

A sail is never fashioned absolutely flat. The sailmaker, by gathering, cutting and sewing the cloths that make up a sail, creates a curve in the finished product something like the curve in an airplane wing. The windward side of a hoisted sail is concave and the leeward side is convex. This applies to all sails, regardless of their shape, size or use, though some may be shaped flatter or fuller than others.

The wind, as it strikes the luff of the sail, splits as it is turned from its direct course. Some of the wind flows to the windward side and some to the leeward side of the sail.

Since the curve or shape of the sail on the windward side is concave, it therefore has a retarding effect on the wind passing over it. This action builds up a pressure.

The curve on the leeward side is convex. This convex shape allows the flowing wind to pass over the sail quicker than it can on the windward side. The wind, having some-what more distance to travel, is accelerated. This speed-up reduces the pressure on the leeward side of the sail.

So, on the windward side we have an increased pressure and on the leeward side a decreased pressure.

This difference in pressures on opposite sides of the sail creates forces that move the boat upwind, the force on the windward side pushing against a lesser force on the leeward side. It has been said that this lesser or negative force con-tributes as much as $\frac{3}{4}$ of the driving force when close-hauled.

The jib, besides furnishing additional drive in itself, is also an important factor to the forces working on the main-sail. Through the controlled flow of wind over the jib, the speed of the wind flow over the convex side of the mainsail is smoothed out and increased, thereby reducing the lee-ward pressure still more than when sailing with mainsail alone. It is similar to a broad force of wind passing through a narrow slot.

It is most important that the mainsail be set at its proper angle to the wind and the course sailed, and that the jib be properly trimmed to cause the wind to flow evenly and swiftly to create a maximum drive.

It is also important that the jib be set at a proper angle to the mainsail so as (1) not to backwind the main and thus interfere with the smooth wind flow or (2) to be of no help at all to the wind flow. The first is caused by trim-ming the jib in too flat, or by its having an inward curving or a loosely fluttering leech. These disturbing conditions cause a fluttering or luffing in the mainsail, thereby slowing the boat's progress. The second is caused by allowing the jib to set too far out from its proper position.

The same conditions, although forces on the leeward side of the sail are not as strong, apply when sailing on a close reach, a broad reach, or a run. The wind must be allowed to slip off the headsail so as not to interfere with the natural pressures working on the leeward side of the mainsail. Whenever possible they should aid in reducing pressures on the leeward side.

Sails, when set in proper relation to one another, impart maximum drive to the boat.

HOW IMPROPER TRIM OF THE JIB AFFECTS THE WINDFLOW

This drawing shows how the flow of wind on the leeward side of the mainsail is affected when the jib is eased off too far. The wind's direction is not changed, therefore passes on without increasing speed. Some eddies are also formed. The swift smooth flow of wind (see facing page), so necessary for maximum efficiency, cannot take place when sails are set in this manner.

When the jib is trimmed too flat it causes a backwinding of the mainsail. The diagram shows how the flow of wind is forced against the leeward side of the mainsail, causing ripples in its cloth. These ripples, in turn, affect in a negative manner the flow of wind on the windward side. A tight jib destroys the effective wind on both sides of the mainsail, lessening the driving forces and slowing boat's progress.

This diagram shows what happens to wind flow when (1) there is a loose, flapping leech, or (2) the leech has a hard reverse curve. The negative effect on the wind flow is the same when either of the two conditions exist, so the swift smooth flow that causes a decrease in pressure is destroyed. An irregular, bumpy flow backwinds the mainsail and forms ripples in it. To get maximum drive from the effect of a good wind flow, both the jib and mainsail must be properly formed, smooth in surface and set in a relationship that will induce this even and swift flow.

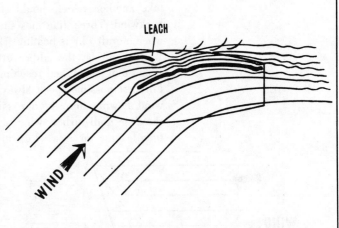

91

The diagram, right, shows the action of wind on a mainsail when the craft is sailing on a beam reach without a jib. Notice the area of agitation behind the sail. Almost all of the force is derived from the push of the wind against the windward side of the sail. The additional force on the leeward side, which should be derived from smooth fast flow, is lost.

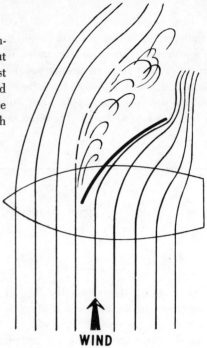

WIND

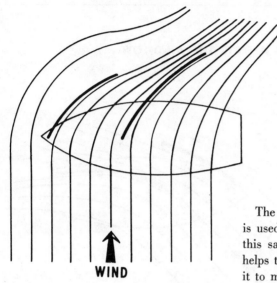

WIND

The diagram, left, shows how the wind flows when a jib is used and set at its proper angle to the main when on this same beam reach. The wind flowing across the jib helps to accelerate the flow behind the mainsail and cause it to move faster, thereby creating an area of lesser pressure which is much desired.

DISTURBED AREAS OF LESS POWER

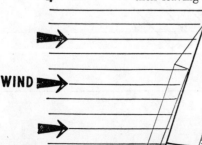

WIND

WIND

1

2

3

WIND

WIND, after passing over the sails, leaves a moving mass of disturbed air. This air is filled with eddies from which most of the drive has been eliminated. It ranges in length from two to four boat lengths. Any craft entering this zone of eddies is unfavorably affected and loses speed. A sailboat seeking to pass or overtake another vessel should stay out of this zone of eddies, or backwind. Three diagrams showing the direction of wind eddies, when a craft (1) is beating, (2) beam reaching and (3) running. When running, the eddies are somewhat wider than the broad expanse of sail. When reaching they are wider than when beating. For best possible speed always try to have free and undisturbed wind flowing across your sails. Diagram (4), a vertical view showing undisturbed wind striking the sails, passing over and then leaving an area of disturbed wind as high as the masthead.

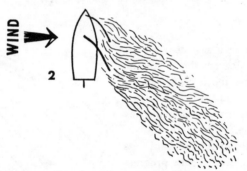

4

WIND

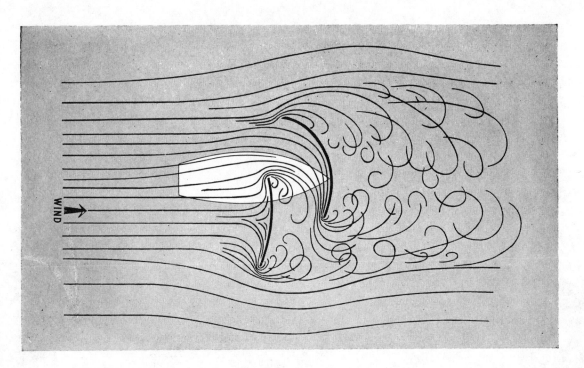

THIS diagrammatic drawing indicates the action of the wind on the mainsail and spinnaker when properly set for running before the wind. In following the wind lines notice how the wind not only strikes both sails directly but some of the wind sliding off the mainsail also works and pushes against the spinnaker. A great driving force is thereby derived when these sails are set in proper rela-tion to each other. To get most out of the spinnaker it must be controlled so it does not backwind the mainsail and destroy that part of the driving force derived by the lesser pressure on the leeward side of this sail. The broad front presented by these sails causes the turbulent mass of air flowing before the craft to be much greater in size than when sailing with the mainsail alone.

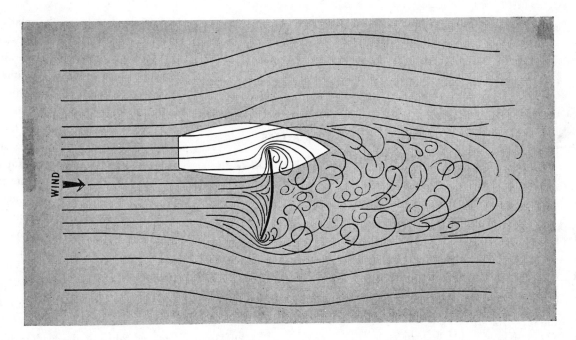

THE above diagram shows the action of wind on the main-sail when running. The greater driving force is on the windward side of the sail. This push contributes approxi-mately ¾ of the driving force, the remaining ¼ coming from the negative or partial vacuum on the leeward side. (These forces are almost exactly opposite to those working when sailing closehauled.) The wind hits the sail broad-side, then pushes out in all directions, up, down and side-ways. It spills over the edges of the sail to form a tur-bulent mass of air that keeps moving ahead of the boat and extends forward from two to five boat lengths. Very little driving force is furnished by the jib, which is omitted from the diagram. Blanketed by the mainsail, it flaps around, only now and then filling or holding wind, unless held out by a boom. It is influenced by the eddies of wind formed in back of the mainsail but it can act, and often does, as a telltale indicating a change of wind by suddenly filling.

This unusual photograph clearly shows the effect of disturbed wind on a craft, #2218. From its upright position and the shivering of the mainsail it clearly shows that it is not getting the strong clear wind that the other boats are enjoying. It is in the zone of eddies and disturbed air. The four boats to windward of it are all pointing high to avoid slipping into the wind streams of the craft ahead. They have good clear wind, though the craft in lead is suffering from a temporary lapse by the helmsman who is not steering his craft as close to the wind as he might. #6700 at the far right, is clear of the wind eddies, but must keep up its speed, otherwise find itself in a predicament similar to that of #2218.

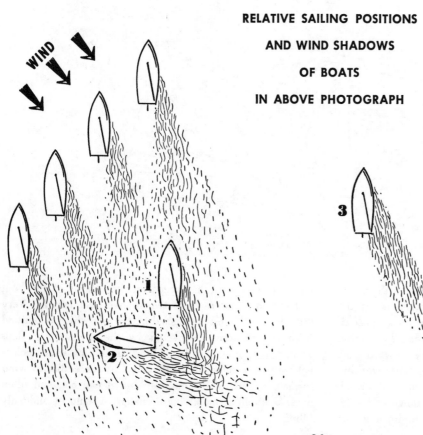

RELATIVE SAILING POSITIONS

AND WIND SHADOWS

OF BOATS

IN ABOVE PHOTOGRAPH

A PLAN view shows the relative positions of sailing craft at the start of a race. The four lead boats are in a safe sailing position and unaffected by the wind flow from the boats ahead. The craft in position #1 is in the worst possible position for a racing boat to get into. She will slow down and soon will be left far astern. To get out of this predicament she should immediately come about, as at #2, sail clear of the adverse eddies of the leading boats, then come about again to windward of them. #3 is all right but must continue to sail fast to remain clear of the retarding air. #4 should adopt the tactics of #2, that is, come about to clear the disturbed wind of the leading boats. A sailing fleet creates an area of disturbed air that is much greater and longer in length than that created by any single craft. Its cumulative effect is shown by the large disturbed area in the diagram. A fleet has been known to affect wind as much as ½ mile to leeward.

The importance of WIND VANES

CHAPTER 30

Wind vanes, telltales and wind pennants are of fundamental importance to all sailboats, for they give you the angle of the wind to the course you are sailing and so indicate how to set your sails or decide the course to sail. When under way, these wind indicators do not indicate the true wind, but give a most helpful relative indication, because of the boat's forward motion through the water. They indicate the true wind direction only when lying at anchor, at the mooring, or when sailing directly before the wind. They are mounted at the mast head or tied to the shrouds.

The masthead vane is of first importance because it has clearer wind, influenced only by the wind itself and the motion of the boat, whereas the other telltales tied to the shrouds are influenced by deflected currents and back winds from the sails. Many skippers sitting on the leeward side of the craft watch the luff of the jib when beating with only an occasional glance, as a check, at the wind vane. On the other points of sailing the wind vane is most carefully watched and the sails adjusted to its varied movements.

The sketch at the right shows the position of the wind vane at the head, or "truck," of the mast and the location of ribbons on the shrouds and backstay. The light, thin ribbons often pick up low level zephyrs that do not register on the vane of the masthead and are most valuable during calms.

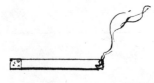

Smoke is moved by the most gentle of breezes. The lighted cigarette is of help in determining wind direction during periods when the breeze is so light it can barely be felt.

HELPFUL HINT . . . The cool side of a wetted forefinger, when held up in the air also indicates the direction from which the wind is coming. This method is often used when the wind is light or variable and barely registers (if at all) on the wind vane. It is also used when sailing at night when the wave direction cannot be discerned and the wind vane not seen without the aid of a flashlight, or fixed masthead light.

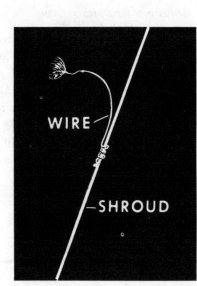

WIRE

SHROUD

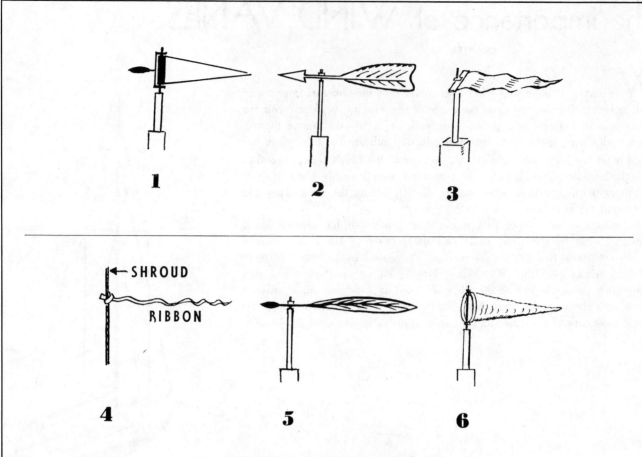

TYPES OF WIND VANES

FIGURES 1, 2, 3 and 5 are masthead swivel-type wind vanes. Figure 3 is of the cloth pennant type which flutters in the breeze, giving wind direction. Figures 1, 2, and 5 are made from very light sheet metal or plastic. Figure 4 is a ribbon or light wool string that is often tied to the shrouds or backstay. Figure 6 is a cloth wind sock. It is a small facsimile of the large red sock used at airports to indicate wind direction to flyers. It *is* sensitive. All types (skipper's choice) are in every day use.

HELPFUL HINTS—

ADJUSTING FORE AND AFT TRIM

Skippers of small cruising craft, where activity is centered in the cockpit aft, purposely adjust the fore and aft trim of their boat so it is "down by the head" when no one is on board. The water line is not level to the horizontal plane of the sea. The stern rides higher than the bow (Figure 1). This is accomplished by placing heavy gear forward. However, the craft levels properly when the crew moves into the cockpit. The weight of the crew, aft, balances the weight forward (Figure 2). The water line then is again parallel to the plane of the sea as it should be for good sailing. This practice is not necessary for the smaller open racing craft or day sailers as the crew can easily be moved forward or aft for proper trim.

How to COIL LINE

CHAPTER 31

Line bought in a ship's store usually comes on large spools and drums. This makes for orderly handling and easy measuring in the store but is not practical on a boat.

When not in use on the boat, line is coiled neatly and compactly, which makes for easy stowage and handling, and prevents kinking, twisting and knotting. These coils are readily made and, what is also important, should the line be wanted in a hurry, quickly unmade.

Manila often has a twist in it which tends to form knots. To overcome this, tow the line astern (be sure you're clear of other boats) for about fifteen or twenty minutes; then haul it in. The twist should be gone. Nylon or dacron does not have to be towed.

Rope, when straight from the drum (as bought in the store) is properly called "rope." When cut into lengths for specific uses it usually is referred to as "line."

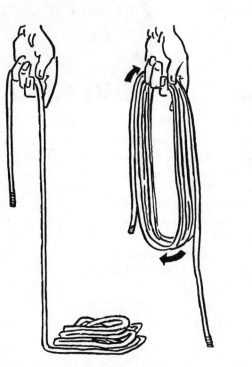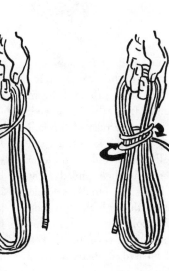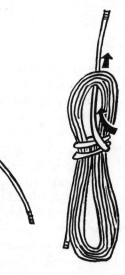

Illustration 1—The common method of coiling for stowing

ILLUSTRATION 1 shows the usual method of coiling line for stowage. The two drawings at the left show how the line is picked up and coiled in uniform loops. The line is handed in a clockwise direction. The pick-up end must hang below what will be the center of the coil. The third and fourth drawings show how the line is bunched by wrapping the loose end around the coils. The fifth drawing, the one on the right, shows how the loose end is then passed through the top loop and pulled tight. When held by this end, the coil stays bunched and can be tossed around.

The photograph, right, shows how a line is handled when being coiled. To make a neat coil, the loops should all be of uniform size. To maintain uniformity, the length of line between the hands should be of equal measure. When making long loops, the hands are stretched far apart. If the loops are to be small, the hands are then kept closer together. The ability to judge the length of line for even loops can be acquired by careful, patient practice. Once the knack of coiling line has been acquired, it becomes easy and can be done rapidly.

Illustration 2—another method of coiling line

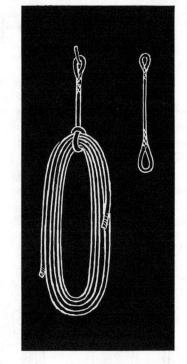

Illustration 3

IN illustration 2, (another method of coiling for stowing) the line is coiled and wrapped with the loose end in the exact same manner as described in illustration 1. From here on, it differs. A loop is made from the loose end. Then the loop is passed through the upper part of the coil as shown in the left-hand drawing. Next the loop is passed over and around the coil and is allowed to fall to the level of the wrap around parts. The end is then pulled tight (third drawing from left). This keeps the bundle set and secure. The loose end is then passed through the top loop and serves as a carrying line. The coil when tied in this manner is less likely to become loose or to ravel than when the previously described method is used. It takes a trifle longer to make or unmake for use.

ILLUSTRATION 3 shows a good method to use when line is to hang on the side of a bulkhead or locker. Here another line is brought into use, a short piece with an eye spliced in both ends (drawing at top right). The coiled line is held and the short spliced piece is passed through its loop. One eye is passed through the other and pulled tight. The eye at the top is now free to serve as a loop for hanging. This makes up into an exceptionally neat, tight bundle that keeps the loops from snarling and kinking.

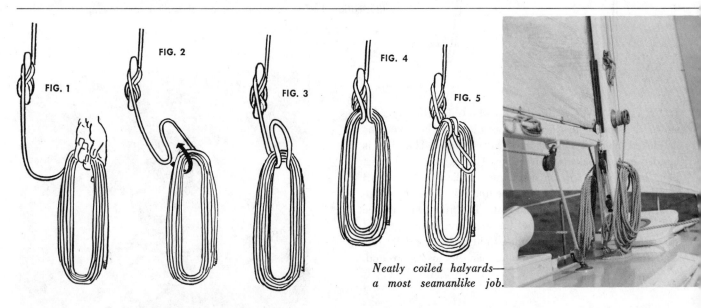

Neatly coiled halyards— a most seamanlike job.

COILING THE HALYARD

COILING a halyard after the sail has been hoisted and the halyard cleated is done in exactly the same manner as previously mentioned in coiling rope for stowage. The line is gathered (Fig. 1) in even loops. When the line between the cleat and the loop gets short a loop is made with the line and passed through the coil as in Figures 2 and 3. The loop is then passed over the cleat on the mast, as

in Fig. 4. For double security the loop can be passed through the coil twice (Fig. 5) and then hung on the cleat. This method is used for coiling halyards on practically all craft where the halyards are cleated above deck and is illustrated in the photograph directly above.

When the sail is to be lowered the coils can be quickly and easily removed from the cleat, and laid on deck where they should run freely without snarling or twisting.

HEAVING A LINE

CHAPTER 32

Heaving a line is one of the elements of seamanship. How it's done distinguishes the experienced boatman from the novice. The latter often coils the line wrong and the end falls short of its mark. The able seaman coils it to run out without fouling and casts it easily.

A few preparations, plus practice, will give you this seaman's touch. To achieve it, here are four essentials to remember.

First, the line must be much longer than the distance it is to be thrown. It must not be just long enough or only a trifle longer, but at least half again the distance. Otherwise, when thrown, it will probably fall short.

Second, the line must be looped carefully and evenly, with the draw of the loops toward the hand holding the free end. The loops should be slightly smaller than those made for other purposes. This is done to concentrate the weight of line in the coil. A smaller, heavier bundle can be more easily controlled than a large, loose one. A loosely looped line is hard to throw; generally it fouls, has no carry-through, and will fall as a snarled lump.

Third, the coil must be held right for throwing. Hold the free end of the line (not the heaving end) in one hand. In the other hand, hold the coil low, at full arm's length. The line should lead directly from one hand to the coil, without crossing or twisting over the loops. This allows the coils of the loop to open freely as the line runs out.

Fourth, the coil must be thrown properly, at the right moment, and at not too great a distance. In an underhand motion, swing the throwing arm back (the one holding the coil); then throw with a stiff arm, achieving a strong, swinging movement. When the coil is released, the arm should be well up above the shoulders. Aim at the head and shoulders of the person receiving. If the aim is at his feet or waist, the line is apt to fall short. Always give the receiver a good chance to catch the line.

If you are throwing to a person on a wharf high overhead, put extra effort into the heave—not just enough to reach the wharf, but enough to reach higher than the shoulders of the receiver, permitting him to reach out to grab the line and haul it in.

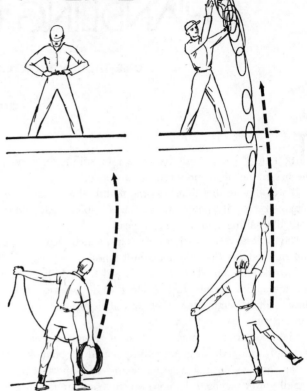

When heaving a line to a spot high overhead be sure to use enough effort to reach as high as the receiver's head.

NAVY METHOD OF HEAVING A LINE

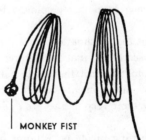

MONKEY FIST

HAWSER

Here the line is divided into two parts. The entire part having the monkey fist is thrown through the air and stays as a single mass until the other part, attached to the hawser, has run out.

Proper throwing stance with the tightly coiled line in throwing hand. The coil is swung in a stiff arm manner and not released until the arm reaches a point above the head and points toward the receiver.

HANDLING the MULTIHULL

SOME THOUGHTS ON CATAMARANS AND TRIMARANS

CHAPTER 33

THE EARLY 1960's will be known in sailing history as the beginning of an important phase in yachting.

It was during this time that the multihull sailboat began demonstrating its potential, and was rapidly adopted in both day-sailing and cruising types.

Day-sailers were mostly catamarans, which proved faster and more stable than the monohull types.

Two factors contribute to speeds which would have been considered impossible just a short while before. One of these is light weight; the other stability—forming a perfect combination for great efficiency.

Light construction means that for a given sail area there is simply more driving power per pound of boat—which is the same as putting a larger engine in a sports car.

Sail power means little, however, unless there is sufficient stability to make the sails effective.

The wide beam (usually about half the length) of the catamaran supplies the stability necessary to keep the mast erect and therefore expose the sails to the full force of the wind.

Another surprising factor was the discovery that thin, slicing hulls are much faster than planing shapes on such a sailboat—just the opposite from power craft.

Handling Is Similar

As far as actual handling of the catamaran is concerned, there is little technical difference from that employed for monohull day-sailers.

Although it was first thought that catamarans were difficult to maneuver, it has been ascertained that the difference is mostly one of technique—plus the fact that early catamarans lacked certain design developments which have since furnished hulls which by their very nature are easier to turn.

While a catamaran while turning pivots on a point between the hulls and thus centerboards in each hull do furnish a certain amount of drag, putting about becomes a simple and instinctive accomplishment once the fundamentals have been mastered.

Primary consideration while changing tacks is to be certain the boat is already close-hauled and moving nicely through the water—it is of little use to try to put about if the boat is sailing well off the wind or not definitely moving at the time.

Let us change tacks in our catamaran (we are close-hauled):

1. A steady turn into the wind is begun. This is main-tained until the jib begins to flutter—then the rudder is turned until it is at an angle of about forty degrees—the most effective angle.

Note: The rate of turning into the wind is critical. If you turn too slowly the boat will lose speed as sail drive is lost when heading nearly into the wind; there is a point where the sails are apparently drawing but in reality furnishing no drive at all. If you turn too rapidly the rudder acts as a brake and essential momentum is destroyed by drag.

2. As the boat continues to turn—*hold* the tiller (at the 40-degree angle) until the bow is past the eye of the wind, and the jib fills on the other tack.

3. As the boat begins coming into the eye of the wind, the mainsail can be hauled perfectly flat in order to maintain drive as long as possible. However, keeping the mainsail flat after passing through the eye of the wind can spoil the maneuver, causing the boat to weathercock. Release the main sheet as the boat passes through the eye of the wind.

There are some other factors: on a turbulent day, wait for a comparative smooth before coming about—it is useless to turn directly into a breaking sea, for instance.

It may also be necessary to move your weight forward in order to keep the transoms from dragging—which can be a serious handicap at low speeds.

It is also necessary to handle the rudders gently—as they can become brakes as well as steering devices. After some experience the helmsman can feel the point where turbulence begins to form about the rudder blade as he moves the tiller.

If conditions are extreme you can still put about, but with a different technique. In winds so strong that a single-hull boat would be knocked flat, the multihull can still come about.

In this case, it will probably be impossible to complete changing of tacks in the usual manner, as the light boat will gather sternway as soon as it is head to wind.

As sternway begins, the rudders are reversed—and the boat is steered while going backwards so that the head will fall off on the desired tack.

The multihull can also be steered down-wind while proceeding stern-first. This can be an easy way of leaving a dock, etc.

In very light airs it may be necessary to move the crew weight forward so the transoms will not drag in the water, which can cause a good deal of resistance.

As speed increases, crew weight is moved aft—in extreme conditions when it is desired to maintain full speed the crew may be perched clear aft on the windward after-decking.

Sailors accustomed to single hulls must learn to ease sail pressure when the weather hull of the catamaran starts to lift. Not only is the catamaran less efficient when heeled —beyond this stage there comes a point where stability simply disappears and the boat capsizes.

Larger catamarans may be used as cruising vessels, although in such sizes the triple-hull trimaran is appearing in greater numbers.

Modern Double Outrigger

The trimaran is a modern development of the double-outrigger of the Indonesians.

This type makes a particularly safe cruising boat, for when properly designed it can be self-righting and there-fore safe even when heeled at angles far past the point where a catamaran would capsize.

They are usually unsinkable, and shallow draft enables them to utilize waters denied to the usual keel boat.

The trimaran is also comparatively simple to construct, as the spaces between the hulls are relatively short, greatly reducing wracking strains between components.

It is also possible to achieve full headroom in the center section in comparatively small sizes.

Maneuvering the trimaran can be similar to the steps recommended for the catamaran. They are usually also of light construction, and with even greater stability than the usual catamaran are also capable of remarkable speeds.

None of the multihulls roll as do ordinary boats, due to the wide beam and lack of a heavy keel which causes a pendulum action. They usually sail at a small angle of heel, increasing comfort while cruising.

Ranger—a modern, fiberglass racing-cruising catamaran.

41-foot Corinthian cruising trimaran is also fiberglass.

TUNING UP
CHAPTER 34

THE correct masting, rigging, and tuning of sailing craft have puzzled sailors since they, sailors, first went to sea. Most have looked for some hard set of rules—neat formulas —which would end uncertainty once and for all. In 1794, for example, when the frigates of the new United States Navy were being designed, Captain John Barry, who was to command the *United States*, Captain Thomas Truxtun of the *Constellation*, and Joshua Humphreys, the frigates' designer, heatedly debated the masting of the vessels. Each took positions which find analogies among those taken by sailors today. Truxtun, a traditionalist, wanted to follow the tried rule for masting used by the British Navy. Humphreys, an innovator, wanted to break precedent and devise a new rule. Barry, an empiricist, wanted to forget universal rules and mast by trial and error, for, as he wrote during the controversy, if his dimensions worked "it is very easy to find rules for them."

Fortunately modern sailors need not worry about masting their own boats; that is the architect's concern. But they do have to worry about tuning their rigs. And on this topic they will find that present-day "experts" also divide into traditionalists, innovators and empiricists. There are those who favor setting up their boat's standing rigging "bar-taut"; some are firm in their belief that only slack rigging will make a boat go; others just fuss and fret, on and on.

Part of the trouble lies in the incontrovertible fact that boats and masts differ. What may work on a Twelve Meter may not work on a Blue Jay. There are, nevertheless, a number of important points on which traditionalists, innovators, and empiricists agree.

First and most important is that the mast must be straight atwartships at all times. It must not favor one side over the other or there will be a decided difference in the boat's ability to go to windward on one tack or the other. The mast step should be checked to see that the heel of the mast is centered and that it cannot move. If wedges are necessary to hold it firmly, they should be checked for thickness and driven to an equal depth. Take care that the wedges driven in around the mast at the partners are also of an equal thickness and driven to an equal depth. These wedges, incidentally, should be checked periodically throughout the season. They have a habit of working and, if covered by a mast coat and go unobserved from below, may permit the mast to shift its athwartships alignment. One way to make certain that the mast is correctly positioned, and that the masthead is directly over the boat's centerline, is to measure the masthead's distance from each side of the boat. This can be done by running a steel tape measure up to the masthead attached to the main halyard and measuring the distance from a common point. If a steel tape measure is not handy, the halyard itself can be used, but if it has a dacron tail or if it must be extended by tying on a piece of rope, be careful to stretch it evenly.

Next step in tuning is to adjust the upper and lower shrouds so that the mast *remains* straight *when under sail.* The serious part of tuning concerns the boat under sail. It is relatively easy to adjust shrouds so that the mast is straight at the mooring; indeed, the mast should stand straight without the help of shrouds when the sails are not set. The trick is to keep it straight under all conditions.

How hard should the shrouds be set up? Traditionalists, presumably basing their thinking on the dead days of fiber standing rigging, lanyards, and deadeyes, believe in setting up every shroud "bar taut." Before the advent of stainless steel wire and turnbuckles, the bar-taut advocates had a good point for they could never tighten their shrouds to any great extent, certainly never to the point of endangering their rigs by overloading them. Today, however, it is possible to tighten stainless steel shrouds to where something will give way.

I am on the side of the empiricists when it comes to setting up the shrouds. After stepping the mast, driving the wedges, and measuring the masthead distance, tighten the upper shrouds (those leading to the masthead or upper portion of the mast) until they are fairly taut. The lower shrouds should be slacker than the uppers. This will compensate for the stretch of the longer uppers. If the lowers are set up to the same extent as the uppers, stretch in the uppers will allow the masthead to fall off the centerline decidedly. (Do not make the mistake of believing that stain-

Tuning the rigging is only half the key to good performance. A well-scrubbed hull is important, too.

less steel wire does not stretch. It does, in actual practice.) After adjusting the shrouds, adjust the fore-and-aft position of the masthead. Undoubtedly your boat's designer gave thought to the rake of the mast. His solution should be your starting point. Find the rake from the sail plan; then, with a weight—a plumb bob—attached to the main halyard, try to maneuver your mast so that the rake matches that of the plan. (If the plumb bob moves too much for accurate measurement, let it dangle in a bucket of water.) You may have to fuss with the wedges at the heel and partners, but it's worth it. If, incidentally, you want to work on the rake before setting up the shrouds, go ahead, no harm will be done.

The reason I suggest you start tuning the mast's fore-and-aft position by using the architect's plans is that the mast's rake determines in part what sort of helm the boat will carry when working to windward. Presumably the architect has considered the factors which make *your* boat go to weather and has raked the mast accordingly. Follow his rule. If after sailing her a few times in average conditions you find that his attempt at balance doesn't satisfy your requirements, change it. The average boat should have little or no helm in light going. When the wind pipes up there should be some weather helm, but the boat's tendency to head into the wind should not be excessive. If it is, the energy expended by the helmsman in trying to keep her on course will slow her down as well as wear him out. If the weather helm is excessive, rake the mast forward until the helm becomes docile. You may find that your boat will sail fastest and most comfortably with the mast plumb or even raked far forward. There are other factors which may affect the helm. An improperly shaped mainsail, for example, could add to the weather helm.

If your boat has a lee helm, rake the mast further aft; by doing so, that uncomfortable feeling of fighting to keep her up on course—a much more dispiriting condition than fighting a weather helm—should disappear.

After determining the rake of the mast from the sail plan, set up the head- and backstays. (If your mast has jumper stays, they should be set up fairly taut before the mast is stepped, tight enough so that the top of the mast bends forward slighly until the backstay is taken up.) While the shrouds can be slack the stays generally should be taut at all times except when running before the wind. If the headstay is slack the jib will sag off, and its efficiency will be tremendously impaired. If the backstay is too loose, the weight of the jib will tend to make the mast bend forward, and the set of the mainsail will be seriously impaired. Set up the headstay and the backstay so that the mast will be straight when going to windward under your most efficient sails. Set them up bar taut, but remember that there is a limit to everything. Too much strain on the mast will make it bow, a potentially dangerous condition, especially when going to windward in a heavy sea. To prevent some eager crewman from driving the mast through the keel, put stops on the appropriate threads by taping them. And, after the race, it is a good idea to release the tension by slacking off a few turns on the backstay turnbuckle.

Comparatively recently, innovators have found that if the head of the mast is made to bend aft by tightening the backstay, the sail flattens and becomes more efficient when going to windward in a hard breeze. Putting a bend in the mast also tends to tighten the headstay even more, rendering the jib more efficient.

Most large boats and many small ones are now equipped with easily adjustable backstay turnbuckles for this reason. Slacking the headstay in small boats without backstays often has the same effect in a breeze. The head of the mast will bow aft and the draft in the sail will disappear. One warning: make certain that your mast and partners do not need the full support of the headstay to keep from breaking. (If your mast has jumpers and you want to bend your mast aft, tighten them so that the mast is perfectly straight before setting up on the backstay.)

Another reason for using adjustable backstay turnbuckles is that they permit the release of tension when reaching and running before the wind. A boat seems to go much better reaching or running if the mast is not strapped down rigidly. Whether this is because there is more draft in the sail or because the whole rig is less rigid and is able to spring is uncertain. Whatever the cause, it seems to work.

Having tightened the stays it is now time for the emipiricist in you to take over. Go for a sail and try for perfection by trial and error. Pick a day whose winds are most like those you will encounter during the season. In tuning use the sails you will be mostly depending on for the utmost efficiency during the season. Do not make the mistake of going out for a tuning sail shorthanded and using your working jib if you are going to spend the season racing under a large genoa. Have enough manpower to trim your sails efficiently, and have a competent helmsman aboard. The latter is important for the skipper now should spend his time alternately sighting up the mast and adjusting shrouds and stays. These are too important to be left to the affable fellow who came along for the ride.

Before making adjustments to the shrouds after sailing one one tack, try the other tack. See if whatever was wrong on the first is also wrong on the second. Then make the adjustments, and make them gradually—a turn or two at a time. "Adjustment" does not always mean tightening. Loosening may be what's needed. Sight up the mast after each adjustment. Work only on one change at a time so that you can tell just what effect the change has had.

After you get your rig the way you want it, bend over the cotter pins, or safety-wire each turnbuckle. Then tape these devices to protect the sails. Unfortunately, tuning is not over for the season, even after all these measures have been taken. Especially if you race. Each time you go out you should check your mast again. Wire stretches; temperature and humidity may make a difference in your mast; wedges work loose. Racing skippers should try to find competition before the regular season begins to see whether their boats are really tuned or whether it is their imagination that has taken hold. And if you do get your boat perfectly tuned—if you do reach that never-never land—remember the words of Captain Thomas Truxtun: "We ought never to forget to give *Mr. Chance* his proportion of credit for it."

CHAPTER 35

GLOSSARY of NAUTICAL TERMS

To the one who has never sailed before or been around boats, nautical terms and their meanings are very strange and unusual. But to the sailor they are usual and meaningful. These terms have been handed down through the centuries and are only a few that have remained since sails have disappeared from the high seas. They were once everyday words in all coastal towns.

A

ABAFT—A term used to describe the relative position of an object that is farther aft than some other point of reference. Thus the mainmast is abaft the foremast.

ABEAM—At right angles to the keel.

ADRIFT—Loose from its moorings.

AHOY—A term used in hailing a vessel or a boat.

AMIDSHIP—The portion of a vessel midway between bow and stern, also midway between port and starboard sides.

ANCHOR—A device so shaped as to grip the sea bottom. From it a line runs to a vessel so as to hold her in a desired position.

ANCHOR'S AWEIGH—Said of the anchor when just clear of the bottom.

ANCHORAGE—A sheltered place or area where boats can anchor without interfering with harbor traffic. Generally there is a bottom that gives good holding to anchors.

ARM—The part of an anchor extending outward from the crown and terminating at the fluke.

B

BACKSTAY—A wire brace leading from the masthead to the stern.

BACKWIND—When the wind that has passed over one sail hits the back (leeward side, away from the wind) of another sail.

BAROMETER—An instrument registering the pressure of the atmosphere.

BATTEN DOWN—To make water tight, said of hatches and cargo.

BATTENS—Long, thin, narrow wooden strips of wood that are placed in pockets sewn perpendicular to the leech of a sail. They keep the leech flat.

BEAM—The greatest breadth of a boat, usually amidship.

BEAM SEA—A sea at right angles to a vessel's course.

BEAR A HAND—To hurry.

BEAR OFF—To sail away from the direction from which the wind comes.

BEAT—To sail toward the direction from which the wind blows by making a series of tacks while sailing close-hauled.

BEFORE THE WIND—Sailing with the wind from astern—in the same direction toward which the wind is blowing.

BELAY—(1) To make fast to a pin or cleat. (2) To rescind an order.

BELAYING PIN—A wooden or iron pin fitting into a rail upon which to secure ropes.

BELOW—Beneath the deck.

BEND—To fasten a sail to the boom and mast.

BERTH—A vessel's place at anchor or at a pier or quay.

BETWIXT WIND AND WATER—The part of the vessel at or near the waterline.

BIGHT—Any part of a rope except the end; usually refers to a loop in a rope.

BILGE—That part of the inside hull above and around the keel where water will collect.

BILL—The tip of an anchor fluke.

BINNACLE—The stand in which the compass rests and which contains the compensating magnets.

BITTER-END—The last part of a rope or the last link in an anchor chain.

BLANKETED—When a sail is between the wind and another sail, the latter cannot get wind and is said to be blanketed. One boat can blanket another boat by sailing between it and the wind.

BOLLARD—An upright wooden or iron post on dock to which hawsers may be secured.

BOOM—Pole or spar attached to the mast to which foot (lower edge) of sail is fastened.

BOOM CROTCH—A board with a notch cut in one end, into which the boom drops snugly.

BOS'N'S-CHAIR—The piece of board on which a man working aloft is hoisted.

BOW CHOCKS—Metal fittings at the bow, having openings through which a line (generally an anchor or dock line) is passed.

BREAK OUT—To unfurl—to remove from its storage place.

BREAKWATER—An artificial embankment to protect anchorages or harbor entrances.

BRIGHTWORK—Brass or chrome that is kept polished. Bright woodwork is that which is kept scraped and varnished in natural wood.

BROAD REACH—Sailing with the wind coming from any direction from abeam to on the quarter.

BY THE LEE—Sailing before the wind, with the wind coming from the same side the boom is on, dangerous because the wind may get behind the mainsail and cause an accidental jibe.

BULKHEAD—Transverse or longitudinal partitions separating positions of the ship.

BUNK—A built-in bed on board ship.

BUNTING—Flag material or flags collectively.

BUOY—A floating marker anchored to the bottom to indicate a position on the water.

C

CABIN—The enclosed space of a decked-over small boat.

CABLE-LENGTH—100 fathoms or 600 feet.

CAMBER—The difference in horizontal athwartships level of a vessel's deck, highest on the center line.

CARRY AWAY—To break or tear loose.

CARRY THROUGH—The forward movement of a craft after it has luffed.

CAST OFF—To let go.

CAULK—To fill in the seams with cotton or oakum.

CAULKING OFF—Sleeping.

CENTERBOARD—A movable plate generally made of metal that can be raised or lowered through the keel of a boat. The centerboard imparts stability and helps to prevent leeway.

CENTERBOARD BOAT—A sailboat in which a movable plate (centerboard) can be raised or lowered through the keel.

CHAFE—To wear the surface of sail, rigging or spar by rubbing.

CHAFING GEAR—A guard of canvas or rope around spars or rigging to take the chafe.

CHAIN LOCKER—A compartment forward where the anchor chain or line is stowed.

CHARLEY NOBLE—The galley smoke-pipe.

CHECK—To check a line means to keep its movement under control.

CHOCK—A heavy wooden or metal jaw-shaped fitting secured in a rail or on a pier for leading lines or cable.

CHOP—Short, irregular waves.

CHOW—Food.

CLEAT—A horned fitting in wood or metal to which lines are made fast.

CLEW—The lower after corner of a sail.

CLOSEHAULED—Sailing close to the wind.

CLOSE REACH—Sailing with sheets eased and the wind forward of the beam.

COCKPIT—The box-like well in a boat from which the skipper and crew operate.

COIL—To lay down rope in circular turns.

COME UP INTO WIND—Steer toward the direction from which the wind is coming.

COMING ABOUT—Bringing the boat from one tack to the other when sailing on the wind.

CONNING—Directing the steering by orders to the steersman.

CORDAGE—A general term for rope of all kinds.

COUNTER—The side of a vessel's quarter.

CRADLE—A stowage rest for a boat.

CRINGLE—A ring sewn into the sail through which a line can be passed.

CROWN—The point at which the shank joins the arms of an anchor.

CROW'S-NEST—The platform on the mast for the lookout.

D

DAVIT—A curved metal spar fitting in a socket on deck and projecting over the side or stern for handling a boat or handling weights. Sometimes used forward to assist in bringing the anchor aboard.

DAVY JONES' LOCKER—The bottom of the sea.

DEAD LIGHT—A heavy circular glass lens set flush and permanently into decks of bulkheads for admitting light or permitting observation.

DEAD WATER—The eddy of a vessel's wake under the counter.

DEEPS—The fathoms of a lead line which are not marked.

DEEP SIX—A term meaning to dispose of by throwing over the side.

DERELICT—An abandoned vessel at sea.

DINGHY—A small handy rowing boat sometimes rigged with a sail.

DIP—A position of a flag when hoisted part way of the hoist; to lower a flag part way and then hoist it again.

DISPLACEMENT—The weight of the water displaced by the vessel.

DITTY-BAG—A small bag for stowing small articles.

DITTY-BOX—A small box with a hinged lid used for stowing small articles.

DOG WATCH—One of the two-hour watches, between 4 and 8 pm: from 4 to 6 pm is the first dog watch, and from 6 to 8 pm is the second dog watch.

DOLPHIN—A cluster of piles for mooring.

DORY—A small flat-bottomed boat, with sharp bow and tapering stern, used by fishermen and is especially seaworthy.

DOUBLE UP—To double a vessel's mooring lines.

DOWSE—To take in or lower a sail; to put out a light.

DRAFT—The depth of water to a vessel's keel.

E

EASE OFF—To slacken.

EASY—Carefully.

EMBARK—To go on board.

ENSIGN—(1) The national flag. (2) A junior officer in the U.S. Navy.

EVEN KEEL—Floating level.

EYE OF WIND—The exact direction from which the wind is coming.

F

FAKE—A single turn of rope when a rope is coiled down.

FAKE DOWN—To coil down a rope so that each fake of rope overlaps the next one underneath, and hence the rope is clear for running.

FATHOM—Six feet.

FENDER—Canvas, wood or rope used over the side to protect a vessel from chafing when alongside another vessel or wharf.

FLARE—The outward and upward curve in the form of a vessel's bow.

FLEMISH DOWN—To coil flat on deck, each fake outside of the other beginning in the middle and all close together.

FLOTSAM—Floating wreckage or goods.

FLUKE—The flattened end of an anchor arm. (Also called a palm.)

FOG BOUND—Forced to remain in port because of fog.

FORE AND AFT—In the direction of the keel.

FORE PEAK—The part of the vessel below decks at the stem.

FOUL—Jammed; not clear.

FOUL ANCHOR—Said of an anchor when the cable is twisted about it.

FRAME—The ribs of a ship.

FREEBOARD—The distance from the waterline to main deck or gunwale.

G

GADGET—An unseamanlike term used when the correct term is forgotten.

GALLEY—The ship's kitchen.

GANGWAY—An order to stand aside and get out of the way; a platform and ladder or stairway slung over the side of a ship.

GEAR—The general name for ropes, blocks, and tackles, etc.

GILGUY—A term applied to objects whose name is unknown, that do not have a particular name. Also known as a gilhickey, gimmick, gadget.

GIMBALS—A pair of rings one within the other and with axes at right angles to one another for supporting the compass and maintaining it horizontal.

GIVE 'WAY—In rowing, an order to begin rowing.

GRAPNEL—A small anchor with several arms used for dragging purposes.

GROUND SWELL—The swell encountered in shoal water and which is practically constant.

GROUND TACKLE—A term used to cover all of the anchor gear.

GUNWALE—The upper edge of a vessel's or boat's side.

H

HALF-MAST—The position of a flag when hoisted half way.

HALYARD—A line used to raise the sail.

HAND LEAD—A lead of from 7 to 14 pounds used with the hand lead line for ascertaining the depth of water in entering or leaving port.

HAND OVER HAND—A term used in gathering a line or sheet with one hand alternating over the other in short lengths. Often several parts of a sheet are gathered at one time.

HANDSOMELY—Carefully, not necessarily slowly.

HAUL—To pull.

HEADWAY—Moving ahead.

HEAVE—To throw. The rise and fall of a vessel in a seaway.

HEAVE IN—To haul in.

HEAVE SHORT—To heave in until the vessel is riding nearly over her anchor.

HEAVE TAUT—To haul in until the line has a strain upon it.

HEAVE THE LEAD—The operation of taking a sounding with the hand lead.

HEAVING LINE—A small line secured to a hawser and thrown to an approaching vessel or to a pier, for a messenger.

HEEL—To tip to one side; list or inclination.

HELM—The tiller.

HELMSMAN—The one who steers the boat.

HOIST AWAY—An order to haul up.

HULL DOWN—Said of a vessel when due to its distance only the spars are visible.

I

INSHORE—Towards the shore.

IRISH PENNANT—An untidy loose end of a rope.

J

JACOB'S LADDER—A rope ladder with wooden rungs used over the side.

JETSAM—Goods which sink when thrown overboard at sea.

JETTISON—To throw goods overboard.

JIB—A triangular sail at the bow of the boat.

JIB SHEET—The line that leads from the lower aft end of the jib to the cockpit. It controls the angle at which the sail is set.

JIBE—Bringing the boat around to the other tack when sailing with the wind aft.

JIGGER—The after mast of a five-masted vessel. The small sail set at the stern of a yawl-rigged vessel.

JURY RIG—A makeshift rig.

K

KEEL—The principal timber that runs fore and aft along the center line of a boat.

KEEL BOAT—A craft with a fixed keel that extends below the hull.

KEEP HER SO—An order to steady on the course.

KING SPOKE—The upper spoke of a wheel when the rudder is amidships, usually marked in some fashion.

KNOCK-OFF—To stop, especially to stop work.

L

LANDLUBBER—The seaman's term for one who does not go to sea.

LANYARD—A rope made fast to an article for securing it, i.e., knife lanyard, bucket lanyard, etc., or setting up rigging.

LAY—(1) A preliminary order, like: lay aloft, lay out, etc.; (2) The direction of the twists of strands of a rope.

LAZARETTE—A low head-room space below decks in the after part of some ships, used for provisions or spare parts.

LEEWARD—(Pronounced loo'ard)—The direction away from the wind.

LEEWAY—Drift to leeward or in the direction toward which the wind is blowing when sailing.

LONGITUDINAL—A fore-and-aft strength member of a ship's structure.

LUCKY BAG—A locker or compartment for the stowage of loose articles found about the ship.

LUFF UP—Steer the boat so her bow is toward the direction the wind is coming from, thereby causing the sails to shake.

M

MAINSAIL—The sail set abaft the mainmast.

MAINSHEET—The line that controls the angle of the mainsail in its relation to the wind.

MAKE COLORS—Hoisting the ensign at 8 a.m.

MANILA—Rope made from the fibers of the abaca plant.

MARK—The fathoms of a lead line which are marked. The call used in comparing watches, compass bearings or courses.

MAST—The vertical pole or spar supporting the booms, gaffs and sails.

MASTHEAD—The top of the mast.

MIZZEN—The third mast from forward of a vessel with more than two masts; the after and shorter of two masts in a yawl or ketch.

MONKEY FIST—A knot worked into the end of a heaving line.

MOORING—Large anchor permanently in position (generally in a mooring area) to which are attached chains and line leading to a floating buoy.

MOORING FLOAT—A floating buoy, like a spar or a can, used to mark the position of a permanent mooring.

MOORING SWIVEL—A large heavy swivel with two links and shackles attached to each of its parts, for use in mooring ship.

N

NOT UNDER COMMAND—Said of a vessel when disabled from any cause.

O

OILSKINS—Waterproof clothing.

OLD MAN—The captain of the ship.

ON SOUNDINGS—Said of a vessel when the depth of water can be measured by the lead—within the 100-fathom curve.

OUTBOARD—Towards the sides of the vessel.

OUTHAUL—A device and line used to haul out the clew or after corner of a sail, when attached to a boom.

OVERALL—The extreme deck fore-and-aft measurement of a vessel.

OVERHANG—The projection of the stern beyond the sternpost, and of the bow beyond the stem.

OVERTAKING—Said of a vessel when she is overhauling or overtaking another vessel.

P

PAD EYE—A metal eye permanently secured to a deck or bulkhead.

PAINTER—A short piece of rope secured in the bow of a small boat, used for tieing up or towing.

PART—To break.

PAY OUT—To slack out on a line made fast on board.

PEA—The tip of an anchor fluke, also called the bill.

PELICAN HOOK—A hinged hook held together by a ring. When the ring is knocked off, the hook swings open.

PENNANT (or pendant)—A length of rope with a block or thimble at the end.

PIPE DOWN—An order to keep quiet.

PIVOTING POINT—The point in a ship about which she turns.

PORT SIDE—The left side, facing the bow from aft.

PORTUGUESE MAN-OF-WAR—A jellyfish with a sail-like protuberance above water.

PRIVILEGED VESSEL—One which has the right of way.

PROLONGED BLAST—A blast of from 4 to 6 seconds' duration.

PUFF—A sudden burst of wind stronger than what is blowing at the time.

Q

QUARTER—That part of a craft that lies within 45° from the stern, known as the starboard quarter or port quarter, depending on whether reference is to the right or left side.

QUARTERING SEA—A sea running toward either quarter of a craft.

R

RAKE—The angle of a vessel's masts from the vertical.

RAKISH—Having a rake to the masts; a smart, speedy appearance.

REACH—To sail from points between closehauled and running.

READY ABOUT—An expression used to indicate that the boat is about to tack.

REEF—The rolled-up part of a sail tied with the reef points.

REEFING—Reducing sail area.

REEF POINTS—Short pieces of line, fastened to the sail, used for tying a reef.

RIBS—The frames of a vessel.

RIDE—To lie at anchor; to ride out—to safely weather a storm whether at anchor or underway.

RIGGING—A general term applying to all lines, stays and shrouds necessary to spars and sails.

RIGHT—To return to a normal position, as a vessel righting after heeling over.

RINGBOLT—A bolt fitted with a ring through its eye, used for leading running rigging.

RISE AND SHINE—A call to turn out of bunks or hammocks.

ROLLERS—Long swelling waves moving with a steady sweep.

ROUGH LOG—The ship's log as written up in pencil by the quartermaster and the officer-of-the-deck.

RUDDER—A movable, flat device hinged vertically at the stern of a boat as a means of steering. It is controlled by the tiller or wheel.

RUNNING—Sailing with the wind from astern or on the quarter.

RUNNING RIGGING—The part of a ship's rigging which is movable and rove through blocks, such as halyards, sheets, etc.

S

SAIL HO!—The hail from a lookout to notify that a vessel has been sighted.

SCOPE—Is the length of anchor line measured from the bow chocks to the anchor on the sea bottom.

SCULLING—Moving the tiller back and forth quickly to move the boat ahead.

SCUPPER—Opening in the side of ship to carry off water from the waterways or from drains.

SCUTTLEBUTT—The container of fresh water for drinking purposes and used by the crew; formerly it consisted of a cask; gossip.

SEA ANCHOR—A drag (drogue) thrown over to keep a vessel to the wind and sea.

SEA DOG—An old sailor.

SEA-GOING—Capable of putting to sea.

SEA LADDER—A rope ladder usually with wooden steps for use over the side.

SEA LAWYER—A seaman who is prone to argue, especially against recognized authority.

SEAWAY—A place where a moderate or rough sea is running.

SEAWORTHY—Capable of putting to sea and able to meet usual sea conditions.

SECURE—To make fast; to make safe.

SECURE FOR SEA—Extra lashings on all movable articles.

SEIZE—To bind with a thin cord, like seizing the end of a rope or seizing two ropes or ends of ropes together.

SET TAUT—An order to take in the slack and to take a strain on running gear preparatory to heaving it in.

SET THE COURSE—To give the steersman the desired course to be steered.

SHACKLE—A U-shaped piece of iron or steel with eyes in the ends, closed by a shackle pin.

SHAKEDOWN CRUISE—A cruise of a newly commissioned ship for the purpose of training the crew and testing all parts.

SHAKING OUT—Untying a reef.

SHANK—The long part of an anchor between the ring and crown.

SHEAVE—The wheel of a block over which the fall of the block reeves.

SHEET—Is a line that controls the angle of the sail in its relation to the wind.

SHEER OFF—To bear away.

SHIPSHAPE—Neat, seamanlike.

SHOOTING UP INTO THE WIND—Steering the boat into the eye of the wind under its own maximum momentum.

SHORT STAY—When the scope of chain is slightly greater than the depth of water.

SHOVE OFF—To leave; to push a boat away from a pier or vessel's side.

SIGHT THE ANCHOR—To heave an anchor up to the water's edge to make sure it is clear; it is then again let go.

SINGLE UP—To bring in double lines so that only single parts remain secured.

SING OUT—To call out.

SISTER SHIPS—Ships built on the same design.

SLACK—Not fastened, loose. To ease off. The state of the tide when there is no horizontal motion.

SLACKENED—Loosened.

SMALL STUFF—Small cordage designated by number of threads or special names, such as ratline stuff, marline, etc., usually of American hemp, tarred.

SMART—Snappy, seamanlike; a smart ship is an efficient one.

SNARL—To tangle.

SNUB—To check suddenly.

SOUNDING LINE—A line marked to measure the depth of water. Attached to the end is a weight or lead. Often called a lead line.

SOUTHWESTER—An oil-skin hat with broad rear brim.

SQUALL—A sudden and violent gust of wind often accompanied by rain or snow.

STANDING PART—The fixed part of a rope—the long end when tying knots.

STANDING RIGGING—That part of a ship's rigging which is permanently secured and not movable, e.g.: stays, shrouds, etc.

STARBOARD—The right side, facing the bow from aft.

STEERAGE WAY—The slowest speed at which a vessel will steer.

STERN—The after part of a boat.

STERNPOST—The aftermost vertical timber or casting and fitting into the after end of the keel.

STOCK—The crosspiece of an anchor. When in fixed position, in use, it is at right angles to the shank.

STOP—A piece of line or a canvas strap used in tying a rolled-up or gathered sail.

STORM JIB—A small triangular sail at the bow of the boat, used in very heavy weather.

STOVE—Broken in.

STOW—To put in place.

STRAKE—A continuous planking or plating fitted end to end from stem to stern of a vessel's side.

SWAB—A rope mop.

SWAMP—To sink by filling with water.

SWING SHIP—The evolution of swinging a ship's head through several compass points, to obtain compass errors for making a deviation table.

T

TAR—A sailor.

TARPAULIN—Heavy canvas used as a covering.

TAUT—With no slack; strict as to discipline.

TEND—To man.

THREE-SHEETS IN THE WIND—Well under the influence of liquor.

THWART—An athwartships seat in a boat.

THWARTSHIPS—At right angles to the fore-and-aft line.

TIDE—The rise and fall of the sea level caused by the gravitational forces of the moon and sun. This causes the inflow and outflow of waters adjacent to land.

TILLER—A wooden bar used to turn the rudder.

TOPPING LIFT—A rope used for topping up a boom and taking its weight.

TOPSIDE—Above decks.

TRACK—The path of a vessel.

TRANSOM—The athwartships timbers bolted to the sternpost. Stationary couches or settees in a cabin.

TRICE—To haul up.

TRICK—The period of time during which the steersman remains at the wheel.

TROUGH—The hollow between two waves.

TRUCK—The flat circular piece of wood secured at the top of the highest mast or at the top of a flagstaff.

TUMBLE HOME—The amount the sides of a vessel come in from the perpendicular.

TURNBUCKLE—A metal appliance consisting of a thread and screw capable of being set up or slacked back and used for setting up standing rigging.

TURN OF THE BILGE—The point where the frames of a vessel turn from the vertical to the rounding of the bilge.

TWO BLOCKED—When the two blocks of a tackle have been drawn as close together as possible.

U

UNBEND—To cast adrift or untie.

UNDER WAY—Said of a boat moving and under control of the helmsman. (Technically, a vessel is under way when not aground, at anchor, or made fast to the shore.)

UNSHIP—To take apart or to remove from its place.

UP ANCHOR—The order to weigh the anchor and get underway.

UP AND DOWN—Perpendicular.

V

VEER—To slack off and allow to run out; said of a change of direction of wind.

W

WAY ON—The movement of a boat through the water.

WEATHER HELM—When the tiller has to be held off the center line and toward the weather side or wind to keep a boat on its course.

WEATHER SIDE—The windward side.

WINDWARD—The direction from which the wind is coming.

WINDWARD-LEEWARD—A term used in racing when sailing to a marker that is in a direction from which the wind is coming and then back to the starting line.

Y

YAW—To steer wildly or out of the line of the course, as when running with a heavy quartering sea.

A FEW GENERAL TERMS
CONSTANTLY USED WHEN SAILING

When a boat is free or moving away from its mooring or dock it is said to be underway.

The side of the boat that the wind is coming from is called the windward side, and the opposite side is called the leeward side (pronounced looward).

There are three waves created by a boat moving through the water, (1) the bow wave, or the wave formed at either side of the bow; (2) the quarter wave, which is formed at that part of a vessel's side that lies between the stern and beam; (3) the stern wave (also called wake), that runs aft or away from the stern.

Any object that lies forward of the bow is said to be "ahead," and any object that lies in the opposite direction or behind is "astern."

The left side of a boat, looking forward, is known as the port side. The opposite, or right side, is called the starboard side. Originally, it is believed, port side referred to the side of the vessel that was tied to the wharf or pier for unloading or loading of cargo; and starboard referred to the side of the vessel on which a large steering oar was placed. (This was before the rudder came into use.) The front of the boat is called the bow and the rear end is called the stern.